FREDDIE

MY WORLD   ANDREW FLINTOFF

HODDER &
STOUGHTON

Copyright © 2006 by Andrew Flintoff

First published in Great Britain in 2006 by Hodder & Stoughton
A division of Hodder Headline

The right of Andrew Flintoff to be identified as the Author of the Work has been asserted by him in accordance with the Copyright, Designs and Patents Act 1988.

A Hodder and Stoughton book

1

A CIP catalogue record for this title is available from the British Library

ISBN 978 0 340 923894

ISBN 0 340 92389X

Typeset in Akzidenz Grotesk

Printed and bound by
Butler & Tanner Ltd, Frome

Hodder Headline's policy is to use papers that are natural, renewable and recyclable products and made from wood grown in sustainable forests. The logging and manufacturing processes are expected to conform to the environmental regulations of the country of origin.

Hodder & Stoughton Ltd
A division of Hodder Headline
338 Euston Road
London NW1 3BH

ACKNOWLEDGEMENTS

It is difficult to know where to start when it comes to thanking people for getting me where I am today and producing this book.

To start with I want to thank my wife Rachael and two children Holly and Corey for supporting me and encouraging me, no matter how I do on the field. They have also put up with my long absences and disappointments when I have been injured this summer. They are my inspiration.

I also have to give my thanks to Mum and Dad for setting me off in the right direction and supporting me throughout my career. The last twelve months have been great for the Flintoff family, but I owe it all to their support in the early years.

Of course, this book would not have happened without Neil Fairbrother, to whom I owe more than I can say. He has advised me throughout my career and also introduced me to Andrew 'Chubby' Chandler of International Sports Management. Between them they set me back on the right track to the England team and now organise my busy life. I don't know what I'd do without them.

I should also mention the patience and determination of Tom Shaw, whose superb photographs have made this book come alive. Having my photograph taken is not my favourite pastime, but Tom made sure we had a good laugh at all the sessions and I thank him for his hard work. Thanks, too, to Michael Mack for designing the book in such a way that it does look special, and to Gabrielle Allen, for picture consultancy.

Again I am much indebted to my friend Myles Hodgson for making sense of my recollections and managing accurately to convey in writing what I told him over a coffee or two. It has been a pleasure to have him on board.

Last but not least I cannot forget my publisher Roddy Bloomfield. He was the driving force behind the previous book *Being Freddie*, and has been equally encouraging throughout this project. It is a tribute to his enthusiasm and energy that this book has been produced to such a high standard again.

To Rachael, Holly and Corey

CONTENTS

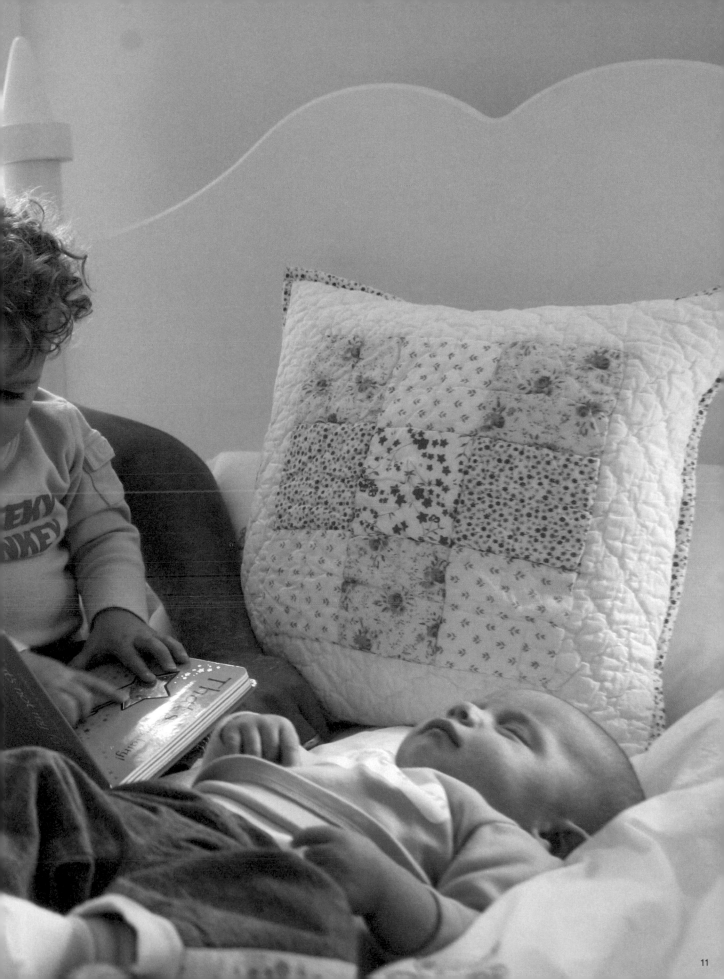

PREFACE

Were you there? Were you one of the thousands of people who were dancing at The Oval when we won the Ashes, or maybe one of the thousands more who were in Trafalgar Square to continue the celebrations? Perhaps you were one of the millions who watched every bit of the drama on television. I know it changed my life forever. Before that memorable series the rest of the squad and I were recognisable only to cricket fans but the country got so gripped by the series that we all became famous.

Then we were invited to Buckingham Palace to meet the Queen after being given awards in the New Year's Honours List. I even got to talk to her on my own for a few moments. When you start playing cricket in your back garden as a kid, the last thing you expect is to end up winning an OBE for doing it and having a reception held in your honour at Buckingham Palace.

So much has happened that it is hard to remember what life was like before the Ashes. The last couple of years have been dominated by that insignificant-looking urn. In this book I've tried to capture the whole roller-coaster ride the calm before the storm that was life before the Ashes, and the whirlwind that has been my life ever since.

Opposite: In the heat of the battle, Michael Vaughan helps me celebrate taking Matthew Hayden's wicket during the Third Ashes Test at Old Trafford.

Top: Consoling Brett Lee after we had just snatched a two-run victory at Edgbaston in one of the greatest Tests ever played. Right to the end, Brett refused to give in and showed what a great competitor he is.

Bottom: This time I'm the one who's frustrated. The look on my face says it all as Australia hang on to secure a draw at Old Trafford.

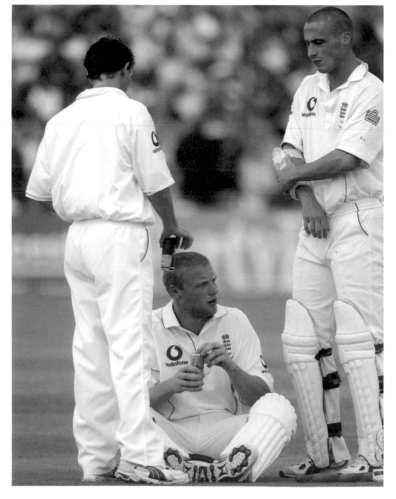

Opposite: No one needs extra motivation when the Aussies come to town, but sometimes I have to boost my energy levels. It's the series both sides most want to win, characterised by all-consuming effort and mutual respect.

Right: Matthew Hoggard and Ashley Giles congratulate each other on winning the game at Trent Bridge against Australia. I've never been so tense, watching them inch us over the line to victory.

AFTER THE ASHES

1

Before we beat Australia, everything we did was regarded as another step towards taking them on, a warm-up for the big event. After each series people would talk about the Ashes to come, so it was massive by the time we actually started playing the Aussies. Everyone was wondering whether England could finally beat Australia and the series seemed to get bigger and bigger while we were in the middle of it. As each Test match progressed, people got more and more excited.

The scenes in Trafalgar Square after winning the Ashes were unforgettable — the scale of the fabulous reception took us all by surprise.

When we won at The Oval and could finally start to celebrate beating Australia in a series for the first time in 18 years, the whole place turned into one big party. Everyone was dancing in the stands. If I had to take one special memory from that summer it would have to be the moment we won the Ashes on that last day at The Oval. It was great being with the rest of the lads on the pitch and looking up to see all our families in the boxes, all the crowds cheering and clapping and everyone loving it.

We genuinely thought we'd be the talk of the town for a couple of weeks and then it would die down and everyone would start talking about something else, but interest in the Ashes does not ever seem to die down. Months later people were still stopping me in the street or in the supermarket to talk about it — I don't think any of us were really prepared for how much it affected people.

I understand the general excitement — I was caught up in it myself. Even though it had been a long summer, I really wanted to keep playing. I was so up for it, I wanted another Test the following week. That series was brilliant to play in and I didn't want it to end. Walking out in front of full houses at every match was something special and I wanted to keep it going for as long as possible, so much so that I can't remember feeling really tired at any point during the Ashes, except perhaps during the Third Test at Old Trafford, but that changed as soon as we got a couple of wickets. It was that kind of series. There was always something to drive you on again. I'll probably look at the DVD of the series in 20 years' time, sitting on my backside with a big belly hanging over my jeans, and wonder how it all happened!

Quite apart from the extra attention, the Ashes gave all the England team a great sense of self-belief. We had taken on and beaten the best team in the world and that gave us a massive confidence lift. We now knew we could beat anyone. I probably thought we were capable of doing so even before we played Australia but, having not played against them personally, there was always a small doubt about whether we could measure up. If I can score runs or take wickets against them, though, I can do it against anyone.

Our victory was not just watched in England and Australia. Cricket is a global game these days and people all over the world watched our performances on television. The teams we have gone on to face have built us up as a side a bit more than they might otherwise have done because of our Ashes win. We were like that ourselves a couple of years ago, building the opposition up in the press and approaching most series as underdogs. Now other teams are doing the same to us and that results in a form of pressure. Everyone expects you to play at the top of your game all the time — the press, the media, the fans. Ultimately, though, the only pressure you really feel is the pressure you put on yourself, and if we are to progress as a side, it's important that we don't put ourselves under unnecessary stress.

We had a bit of a wake-up call when we lost our next series in Pakistan and the talk was of the defeat being an Ashes hangover. I can honestly say we tried our nuts off, but it just didn't happen. I suppose tiredness and fatigue could have played a part. It had been a long year for a lot of us and those Super Series matches I went to play in Australia didn't help. To spend three and a half weeks playing cricket in Australia shortly after the end of the Ashes sounded great at the time but, looking back, I should probably have stayed at home. My ankle started to play up towards the end of the trip — I think my body was tired. I know I felt a lot fresher for having six or seven weeks off before I went out to India after Christmas. I could probably have done with a rest, but I regarded Super Series selection as a major honour, and it was also a good opportunity to play with some of the world's best players. We were soundly beaten by Australia, but that just served to underline that, no matter how good the individuals in a side, it's very difficult to beat a team who have been together for some time. If you look at successful sides, they have usually been built up over time — the side that won the Ashes was probably two years in the making.

My trip to Australia began with the ICC awards for the cricketer of the year. That event was the start of a large number of awards ceremonies for most of us, but the prize I received that night was a genuine surprise to me because I didn't think the time-frame for the awards took in the Ashes. I only went along because I was invited. To receive the ICC Player of the Year award jointly with South Africa's Jacques Kallis was a real honour because I still regard him as the best all-rounder in the world. I know he doesn't bowl that much any more but he's a class act and to share the stage with Jacques and Rahul Dravid was pretty momentous for me.

The really good thing about the Super Series was getting to know players from other teams. Mark Boucher, Graeme Smith and Jacques Kallis are tough opponents in South Africa, and I had wondered what it would be like playing with them instead of against them. I've had a fair amount of stick when I've faced them in the past, particularly Graeme Smith. Virtually every time we've come up against one another we've had a bit of a go. As for Mark Boucher, he's always going at it from behind the stumps, but now I've played alongside them and had a beer with them afterwards, I realise they are not such bad lads. It might even help next time I play against them because once you've shared a dressing room with them you see what players are like. You notice their habits and see the way they go about their business. For all the good things about the Super Series, I did miss the intensity of playing for your country. There is nothing like playing for England. Joining players together from different countries didn't feel the same. Getting Adam Gilchrist out or being hit for four didn't mean as much to me. The same passion wasn't there.

If nothing else, going to Australia got me away from all the fuss back home. Photographers had been following my wife Rachael, daughter Holly and me everywhere and I thought the break would let it all settle down. Not a bit of it. The attention is very flattering, and I suppose I'm stuck with it now, but there are times I wish we could have won the Ashes without getting all the publicity. Going out to Pakistan was almost a blessing. I was able to get back to thinking about cricket and batting and bowling — the things I do best. Of course, I was still recognised in Pakistan and India, because my profile has been raised since the Ashes, and if there's one thing they know about there, it's cricket! They are such big cricket-lovers they had all been following the series, so I was expecting quite a bit of attention. Everywhere we went in Pakistan we had to take security guards with us anyway, and they made sure things went smoothly. If we hadn't had them, we would have been mobbed.

Things had calmed down a bit by the time I got back from Pakistan, and Rachael, Holly and I were able to spend a good five or six weeks together before I flew out again to India. The tour to Pakistan signalled a new start. I could focus on the future after all those weeks and months of thinking and talking about nothing but the Aussies. I thoroughly enjoyed playing in the 2005 Ashes, but there comes a time for everyone to move on. That victory has been the highlight of my career so far but I don't want it to be the only one. I was 27 when we won the Ashes and I'm hoping I still have a few more seasons of playing cricket at the top level in front of me. I'm sure for years to come I'll get people telling me where they were when they watched us at Trent Bridge or Edgbaston, but I'm not one for living in the past.

Even when we were involved in a tough series with Sri Lanka, and my old friend Muttiah Muralitharan, in the summer of 2006, I was still being asked about the Ashes. In the press conference before the Second Test at Edgbaston, questions came up about my memories of the previous year and the incredible game played there against the Aussies. I answered a couple, recalling the 2-run win, but I also told the press I wanted to look forward and not back. Sri Lanka are a talented side and I wanted to concentrate on that match rather than on one that had been played a year ago.

I understand all the attention paid to the Ashes, but I want to go on and play for the best team in the world, and if we are to become that we need to beat teams home and away all around the world, just like Australia have done for so long. I want to beat Australia in their own country and I want to help England win the World Cup. I have plenty of ambition and a lot of things still to do.

I'm quite good at drawing a line under a period of my career and moving on to the next one. When I got back into the side after the World Cup in South Africa, for instance, it was almost like a new start for me. I thought about what had gone before, the struggles I'd had and the battle to get back into the side, and decided to put that all behind me. That's what I'm doing now. This England team is a young one and there is no reason why we can't develop together. The team that took the field for the final Test in Mumbai did not have a single player over 30 and that has got to be good for the future. I hope that the Ashes win is not the pinnacle for this side but the starting point for us to go on and become the best team in the world.

If I had to pick out one highlight from the Ashes it would be that final day at The Oval. The whole ground seemed to turn into one big party.

Top: Just knowing my family is in the crowd supporting me has played a big part in any success I've had.

Bottom: Holly was part of my Ashes celebrations, and came on the bus with Kevin Pietersen and me.

Opposite: Sharing the ICC player of the year award with Jacques Kallis was a great honour. For me, Kallis is the best all-rounder in the world.

Being asked to play for a World XI against Australia, was flattering — and a privilege — but, with hindsight, I could probably have done with a rest. Although I thoroughly enjoyed the World XI games, the desire to win was not as burning as when I'm playing for England.

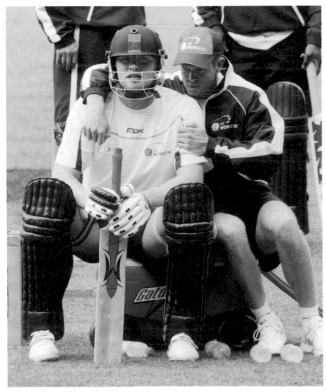

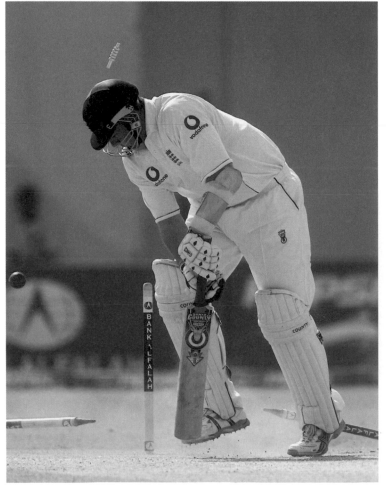

Top: Security was a conspicuous part of our every day lives in Pakistan.

Bottom: Playing on the subcontinent is one of the hardest challenges in world cricket, but we came closer than the scoreline — or this picture — suggests to doing well in Pakistan.

Opposite: Shoaib Akhtar performed superbly during that series against England, demonstrating world-class credentials.

You don't expect to meet the Queen when you grow up playing cricket in the back garden. Meeting Her Majesty with the rest of the Ashes-winning team was a big thrill for me — I was genuinely starstruck!

INDIA AND THE CAPTAINCY

2

Every sport-loving child dreams of captaining the national team. Whether you're a young lad kicking a football around in the park or batting and bowling in the back garden, as I did with my brother Chris, you dream of one day leading out your country. I had the honour of leading England Under-19s, which was a very proud moment for me. It was a job I was surprised to get but I thoroughly enjoyed it, even if I did lead a tour to Pakistan, which is never a favourite touring destination.

When coach Duncan Fletcher asked me to lead the side in India in Michael Vaughan's absence, I was happy to accept.

Ever since then I've harboured ambitions about one day becoming England captain, but with Michael Vaughan doing such a good job, I put the idea firmly to the back of my mind. I've always voiced my thoughts during a day's play anyway, whether I'm playing for Lancashire or England. It's up to the captain whether he takes my opinion into account or not, but at least I'm making a contribution to the side. That was as far as things went until we arrived in India for the start of the tour in February 2006. Michael Vaughan had been forced to return home from Pakistan early because he was having problems with his knee, but an operation was supposed to have sorted it out and he was back to lead us on one of the toughest tours in Test cricket.

However, Michael was clearly still feeling his injury and during a warm-up game in Baroda, I was approached by Duncan Fletcher, England's coach, about the possibility of taking over the captaincy. It was our last game before the First Test at Nagpur and Duncan talked to me about it just as we were starting our second innings. By this stage we knew that Michael's knee wasn't holding up. Duncan told me there was a chance I would be captain the following week for the Test, depending on how Michael's treatment went. He was having a scan and an injection. Marcus Trescothick was on the verge of going home for personal reasons, so I was the obvious choice. With neither of those two being available, I suppose I was the next most experienced player left, so it wasn't that much of a surprise when Duncan approached me.

I was also told I had been an option to captain the side against Pakistan for the First Test in Multan before Christmas, when Marcus got the nod and led the side very well. It was flattering to have been thought of then and I was delighted to be considered in India, but I tried to put it to the back of my mind while we waited to see how Michael bore up during the practice sessions in the days leading up to the First Test. When it became clear that he wasn't going to be fit, I got the official nod from Duncan and, once that happened, I became excited about leading my country and started to look forward to doing it.

Before accepting the captaincy, I had a long chat with Rachael, who was expecting our second child. The plan had been for me to come home after the Second Test in Mohali because the baby was due on 21 March. We always thought it would be early and that's the way it turned out. I'd have loved to have been at Corey's birth, but circumstances were such that it would have been very difficult for me to get there, even without the captaincy. It would have meant Rachael going into labour during a convenient gap between matches, and me jumping straight on a plane for it to happen. The chances of all that falling into place for us were extremely slim to start with. Once I was offered the captaincy, Rachael and I talked it through and we both recognised that this was not an opportunity I could turn down. The only way I could have got back would have been if the baby had been born on the due date, which would have fallen in the break between the Second and Third Tests, but Corey had other ideas.

I wasn't aware of the fuss that was made about our decision that I should stay in India rather than return to attend the birth. Rachael told me there were phone-ins on the radio to discuss the situation and even some of the day-time chat shows were talking about us. One of our friends rang in to a programme called *Loose Women* to defend us without telling the presenters that she knew us. It was amazing that so many people found our business such an interesting subject. We had made a decision as a family, which worked for us, and we were happy with it. What it had to do with radio stations or television programmes I'm not sure.

All the same, I found that period of the tour very difficult. When Corey was born I was absolutely delighted, but it was hard to handle knowing Rachael was back at home with our new son and I was thousands of miles away in India. Pictures of Corey were emailed to me but it was a strange experience having friends who had been around to the house telling me about my own baby before I'd even met him. I almost didn't want to know — it was a tough few days after the birth, being away from it all. As well as not seeing Corey, I was also missing Rachael and Holly. It was great to get back for a few days after the final Test in Mumbai.

Despite these considerable drawbacks it was still an exciting time for me. We had just had a baby and I had been given the England captaincy all around the same time. With everything else going on I must admit I didn't ring my dad to tell him about the captaincy until it was officially announced — I don't make a lot of phone calls when I'm away — but I know he was thrilled about it all. It was almost as exciting a time for him as it was for me, having a new grandchild and one of his sons captaining England.

My family were obviously delighted about the captaincy, but everyone else seemed very concerned about the effect it might have on my game. I was looking at it positively. The rest of the world didn't see it the same way and were talking quite negatively, saying it was bound to be too much of a strain on me, but I couldn't wait to start. As an all-rounder I'm in the game all the time anyway with my batting and bowling and standing at slip, so I couldn't see how captaincy could be that much more of a burden — I was hoping it might bring out the best in me. People may think that when I'm at slip I've switched off and am away with the fairies, but I spend a lot of time thinking about the game, about how I can help the situation or what would improve our position. It wasn't that much of a leap going from that to captaining the side — the only difference was that people suggested things to me rather than the other way around.

I certainly didn't leave the field of play at the end of each day feeling any more tired than I would have been anyway.

I want to be involved in the game all the time and I'm like that no matter who is captain. Sometimes when we're in difficult situations, I'm the first one to volunteer to bowl to help out the team, but once I was captain I had to be semi-sensible about that. I had both Steve Harmison and Matthew Hoggard in my ear telling me if I was taking on too much. I still wouldn't let the fact that I am captain stop me from bowling, though, because the situation should dictate how much I bowl, not my position.

I was very wary of overworking our bowlers in India. Because of the heat and how hard it is to bowl there I tried to keep every bowler down to four or five-over spells. The only time I really felt the responsibility was when I batted. I hadn't played that well in Pakistan, but in India I was batting quite well again. I wasn't trying to belt the ball and hit boundaries all the time. I felt more comfortable playing that way in India. I've worked hard at my game and I was trying to play as I would like, rather than focusing on what it meant to the side for their captain to make runs.

It helped that I had a really good bunch of lads to captain. The circumstances in which we found ourselves — losing Michael Vaughan, Ashley Giles and Simon Jones through injury and Trescothick going home — pulled us together and we rallied. As a team we had a chat about the fact we'd been written off. Everyone was saying we had no chance but we saw it as an opportunity. We gave debuts to Alastair Cook, Monty Panesar and Ian Blackwell in the First Test. It was an opportunity for them to get out there and play Test cricket, and one that might not have come along under normal circumstances. Alastair Cook took his chance and scored a hundred on his debut, while Monty claimed Sachin Tendulkar as his first Test wicket, and he got Rahul Dravid out in the Second Test. So even though everything was stacked against us, in some ways it allowed us just to go out there and play. I never had any doubts that the side would play for me and each other. It was an opportunity for a new-look side, a young side, to compete against India and that's exactly what we did. We believed that we could give a good account of ourselves and that carried us through to a fantastic result. I thought we were magnificent throughout the series.

With everything that happened in the build-up to the First Test, I just wanted the match to get under way. Once we started playing, the atmosphere became totally different. I enjoyed it. It was great to see Alastair Cook, at just 21 years of age, around the dressing room. He's young but he wants to play and he wants to learn, and it is the same with Monty. Although it wasn't the team I had played with for the last year or so, I was excited about the match because all they wanted to do was perform. I had some good mates within the squad anyway and as a side, we each took responsibility for what we were doing. If Harmison or Hoggard come on to bowl, they know what they want, so I didn't really have to do much there. I leaned on that pair a lot during the series and they offered good advice and were really supportive.

In the first session of the First Test at Nagpur we went out to bowl and I was all over the place. I was talking to the bowlers too much and bowling my overs a little more quickly than normal. Steve Harmison took me to one side and told me to calm down and slow down, otherwise I was going to be knackered for the rest of the day. Harmison, Hoggard, Paul Collingwood and Andrew Strauss all put in their two penn'orth, so I had plenty of good advice when I needed it. It was real team effort, everyone pitched in. Even Monty Panesar, who was making his debut, had a very good idea of what he wanted and had all his field placings worked out in his head. I knew Monty from the Academy a few years before, but back then he wasn't the bowler he is now. Even then, all he wanted to do was talk cricket. He'd talk about the Indian team, he'd talk about Sachin Tendulkar, he'd talk about Ricky Ponting, he'd talk about anything to do with cricket. He just loved it and spent his whole time picking everyone's brains about this and that. He wanted to listen and learn and he's not changed all that much.

Two days before the First Test he came to my room, grabbed the notepad by the phone, and went through every batsman in the India team and what field he wanted to set for each one. He also told me things to look out for when he was bowling, what the signs would be if he was getting tired and things like that. I thought that was absolutely fantastic for someone about to make his debut. It made my job as captain a hell of a lot easier, I can tell you! When he got the nod that he was making his debut at Nagpur the day before the game, he was wandering around with a big grin on his face all evening, he was so excited about playing against India the following day. There weren't any nerves or any anxiety, he couldn't wait to get out there. It was the same with Alastair Cook. They weren't hiding or worried about playing. They regarded it as their opportunity to give it a go at Test level and that was a great attitude to see.

To be honest I didn't have a great deal to do as captain. I moved a fielder from here to there every so often, gave a team talk and that's about it. I suppose it helped that I'm a bowler, so I understand what bowlers go through. Bowlers have to accept that runs are going to be scored and they are going to be hit for the odd four or six. They all try their best and sometimes it just works out like that. In that situation I probably have more sympathy for the bowlers than most. In the Second Test at Mohali I remember bowling for a four-over spell when I didn't do particularly well, but it wasn't through lack of trying, so I can understand when a bowler doesn't get it quite right. I know all the lads in this England team are trying their best no matter how it comes out.

Leading out the side for the first time was special and I stuck my chest out a little bit more when we walked out on to the field at Nagpur on the first day. I'd thought about what I wanted to say to the team that first morning, but whether I'm batting, bowling, fielding or captaining the side, most of the things I do are by gut instinct. I'd written a few things down but once I started I just binned it and carried on talking. I spoke from the heart, which I think is the best way for me. If I had stood up in front of the team reading off bits of paper, they'd have looked at me as if I had two heads. I'd sooner say what comes naturally and I'm sure the team react better to that than if I stood there with a prepared speech.

I hadn't really thought about what sort of captain I wanted to be in advance because of the rapid way it came about, so I had to go with my instincts and get on with it. This was very much Michael Vaughan's team and I tried to keep all the ethics he has brought to the side in place until he returned. I didn't try to be too clever. I just cracked on and did the job the only way I know how and, thankfully, the side responded. I was still one of the lads, which I didn't want to change because I like that side of being a cricketer — having a crack with the lads. I don't think it would have helped anyone if I had started detaching myself from the rest of the team. I enjoy being in the thick of it. I still sat at the back of the bus and had the room next to Steve Harmison's. If I'd acted otherwise, it would have been a long and lonely tour, and I'm sure I'd be a much less effective player and captain if I were miserable.

I've played under a few captains for Lancashire and England, but I just tried to do the job my way rather than take little bits from each of them. As long as everybody is trying on the field, there's not much more you can ask, is there? I don't see the point in kicking sods out of the ground or shouting and screaming at everyone when things aren't going right — a Test match would have seemed a very long time if I'd gone round doing that. When Michael Vaughan captains the side he's pretty calm and lets the game unfold in front of him and that's what I tried to do.

I certainly wasn't up all night worrying about who was going to bat at number four or who was going to bowl the opening over the following day — those things aren't going to keep me awake. I can't imagine ever getting to that stage even if I took on the job permanently, although I know some captains, such as Nasser Hussain and Mark Chilton with Lancashire, have gone through phases like that. Being stand-in captain I was spared some of the hassle of selection and handling the media that they had to cope with. I'm sure I made mistakes during my time as captain but I learned quite a lot doing it and tried my best.

Being occupied with the captaincy also helped me cope with missing my family but it was great to fly back for three days to see them after our victory in Mumbai. Holly had grown so much while I'd been away and Corey was nearly three weeks old by the time I met him for the first time. Once again, photographers were camped outside the house, but I had a stroke of luck. I was booked on the shuttle from Heathrow to Manchester, but Paul Beck, whose company LBM are Lancashire's chief sponsor, arranged for his helicopter to pick me up in London. It landed behind the house and I went in the back way. All the photographers were either outside the front door or waiting at Manchester Airport, so for once I dodged them all.

We asked a photographer we knew to take a family picture to distribute to the media, hoping it would stop the rest hanging around the house and following us everywhere we went, but it didn't work. Even when Rachael went to the town hall to register Corey's birth someone popped out with a camera to take a picture of her as she arrived — why would they want to do that?

They say that small kids have no sense of time, so whether I'm gone for a day or eight weeks I'm not sure Holly realises — that's how it appears anyway. When she sees me on the television she points at the screen and shouts. I suppose she doesn't think it's very strange to see her dad on TV at the moment. When she gets older she'll realise it's not something that happens to everyone's dad. For Rachael and me those three days flew by and then I was off to rejoin the tour.

The schedule from then on was manic. Seven one-day internationals in a row is really tough — even five would be a lot, but seven was just unfair. The playing side of it was hard enough, but the travelling didn't make sense either. It wasn't as if we were making a nice pattern around India, we were zig-zagging all the way through. We played, got back to the hotel in the evening and then set off for the next venue the following morning and that routine was difficult for everyone. It was decided I would sit out the final three matches and by that time I was quite glad of the rest. There had been a lot of talk around the squad and in the press about the possibility of resting players. We had already lost the series and it was a good opportunity for me to have a week off.

It was also a good chance to have a look at a few other players. The World Cup is coming up in 2007 and new players need match practice. I'm sure the experience of the Indian tour has helped us get a hell of a lot closer to developing our best team. I know I learned a lot, on and off the pitch, which will help me in the future.

India's captain Rahul Dravid and I share a joke. Leading such a young side on that tour was a pleasure as well as a responsibility.

Leading out the side in Nagpur in my first Test as captain was a proud moment.

Left: Monty Panesar just loves everything about cricket. He walked around with a smile on his face for hours after being told he was making his debut in Nagpur.

Bottom: Monty celebrates after claiming the wicket of Sachin Tendulkar, one of his heroes — his first in Test cricket.

Alastair Cook made a remarkable debut in Nagpur.
He had only been in the country a day or so but was
still able to score a century.

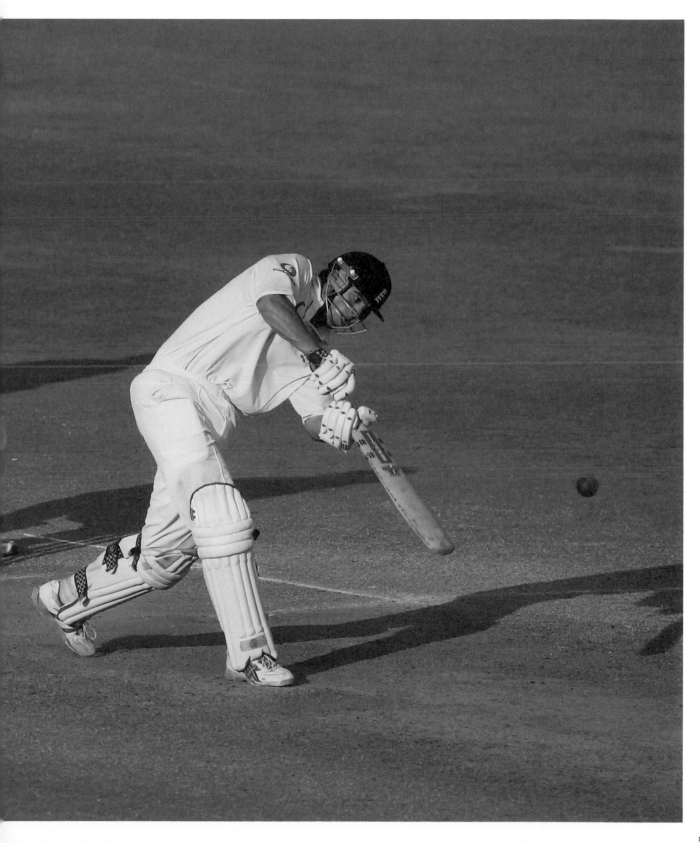

You get to see some
amazing scenes on a
tour to India.

I was fortunate in having quite a few people in the side to turn to for advice — Steve Harmison was particularly supportive.

I'm not quite sure if the fans are agreeing with me or not!

Remaining in India rather than trying to get home for Corey's birth was hard. It was the talk of the town during the Second Test at Mohali.

The passion for cricket in India is legendary. At Mohali, spectators remain glued to the action as Collingwood and Bell face India's spinners.

Checking out the pitch in Mumbai before the
Third Test, which we won — a most satisfying victory.

Walking out for that dramatic final day in Mumbai.

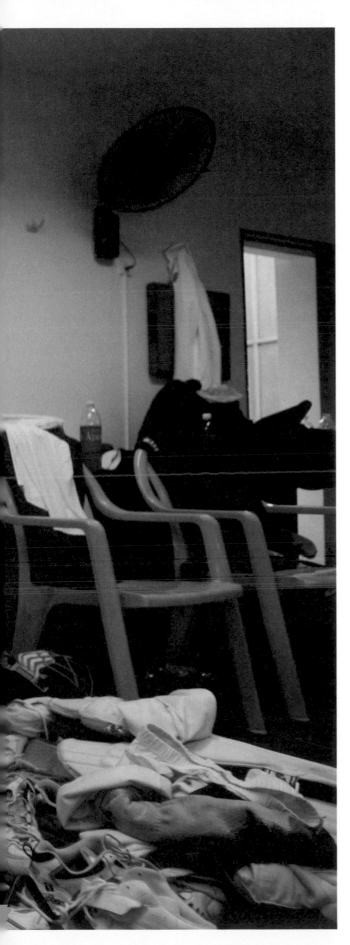

I've always liked mingling with the opposition after a day's play. Rahul Dravid and I chat after the final Test at Mumbai, amid the usual dressing-room detritus.

Chatting with local cricketers in Mumbai shortly before it was confirmed I would take over as England captain.

RUNNING
INTO FORM

3

Fitness has become increasingly important in modern cricket — particularly if you hope to perform at the highest level consistently. My body takes a pounding as an all-rounder. When you bat at number six and are required to bowl quite a few overs, you probably need to be fitter than just about anybody else in the team, and I've been able to perform the way I have done in the last couple of years only because of my increased fitness.

Fitness is an important part of my game. I have to take it seriously if I want to perform at the highest level.

I've always said that if Neil Fairbrother and Andrew 'Chubby' Chandler, who handle all my affairs, hadn't given me a serious talking to back in 2001, I wouldn't be where I am now. My career was at a crossroads. I was out of the England team and struggling for form with Lancashire, so much so that they came to see me at Old Trafford and gave me a right dressing-down. They told me in no uncertain terms where I was going wrong and what I needed to do to get my career back on track. Their criticism was fair and justified, delivered not for commercial reasons but because they genuinely care about me. I accepted what they said and we devised a plan to get me fitter and stronger, to help me improve my game and my consistency. It was a big turning point in my career. As a result of that meeting, I rang Duncan Fletcher and volunteered to go to the Academy, which was then based in Adelaide, for the winter. It was a statement of intent more than anything else, a signal that I wanted to be an international cricketer and was prepared to change my ways to achieve that aim. It was a big surprise to me when, just a few weeks later, I received a call in Australia asking me to join the senior England tour of India to boost their bowling options. I took the chance offered, regained my place in the team and from then on gradually found the consistency I was looking for at the highest level.

When I look back now, I often wonder whether I would have turned my career around on my own without that meeting. Sooner or later I'm sure even I would have worked out where I was going wrong, but it was crucial that things started to happen for me when they did because I was running out of time to salvage my England career. I was gradually realising what I needed to do, but so gradually I was almost at a standstill! If I had carried on like that it could have taken another five or six months and by that time the England selectors could have changed their minds about me. I'd have probably gone on to play county cricket for the rest of my life, averaging 16 with the bat. I was letting down everybody, Neil, Chubby and, mostly, myself, and things needed to change. I'm just relieved the penny dropped when it did, otherwise I don't know where I'd be now.

For all that, I can't help looking back on my time before my lifestyle change with a smile. I had some great moments during that period and behaved like anyone else in their early twenties. The difference was that I was a professional cricketer and couldn't get away with it. I still like to enjoy myself and have a drink, but now I know when to get my head down and concentrate on my cricket and when to go out and have a good time.

Since that period in my life, training has become a major part of my daily routine. I have to stay fit if I am to compete at the highest level and continue playing for England — simple as that. It's something you get used to. I know I have to go to the gym whether

I want to go or not, but I can't say I enjoy it, even now. Some of the guys in the dressing room do not seem to have to train a great deal to stay fit — I just wish I was one of them. I don't mind going running with Dave Roberts, the Lancashire physiotherapist, but lifting weights or pounding along on a running machine in the gym are not my idea of fun. I just see it as part of my job. Dave, who is known as Rooster, and I get on very well and he puts the world to rights while we're working.

I'm often asked how I manage to motivate myself to get up every morning to go off to the gym or meet Rooster to go running and the answer is with difficulty. I know when the alarm goes off I've got to get up and out, but it's not something I want to do. Every morning before I went on tour to India I was training with Rooster and, because of other commitments, I'd have to get up at seven to meet him near Bolton for eight so I could train before doing other things in the day. When the alarm went off each morning all sorts of excuses used to cross my mind to try to get out of it. I thought about ringing him up and telling him I had a headache, but something told me that wouldn't work!

I suppose a lot of the drive comes from wanting to do well for my family and provide for Rachael, Holly and Corey. I want them to be proud of me. If you look at my career, the improvements in my game and the way I go about things coincide with when I first met Rachael. She has run her own company, she enjoys working and enjoys being busy and I don't. A lot of what she's like has rubbed off on me and she supports me in everything I do. I suppose the way I am has rubbed off on her a bit as well. We seem to have found a middle ground — I think she's slowed down and I've speeded up — but I'm still trying to catch up with her. Some people have said it must help having Rachael around to keep pushing me to go training with Rooster, but you should see her. All I get is a 'See you later' before she goes back to sleep!

On my way to meet Rooster, I usually have a high-energy drink to wake me up and another one in the car park while I'm waiting for him to turn up. In a normal training session we do two runs. The first one is to the top of Rivington Pike — we run for a bit and then walk for a bit. It takes around an hour and twenty minutes to get up there and back down again. The other run takes us up another hill to a reservoir, where we run up and down the banks for an hour or so. Depending on what sort of week I've had, after that I'll go to the gym to lift some weights and do some ankle-strengthening exercises, because of the problems I've had in that area in recent years. We also concentrate on strengthening the back, chest and abdominal areas of the body for about an hour and a half.

Everything I do with Rooster is designed to simulate the bowling action so my body is used to it. It works all the muscles I need to bowl without actually running up and bowling, and certainly helps with my stamina. When you've got to come back for one last spell, one last push at the end of a long day, that's when the training tells. I can bowl as well now at the end of the day as I can at the beginning. Rooster has been doing this job for a long time. He was working with the England team way back in the Ian Botham days, so when he talks I listen because he knows his stuff.

The hardest thing about training and getting fit is the boredom and working with Rooster helps me combat that. I'm much better when I train with somebody else rather than on my own. I find it hard to go running or to the gym on my own. If you're training with someone else you let them down if you make excuses and don't do it. I've got a gym at home now. I was going to turn one of the spare rooms into either a gym or a games room and I thought a gym would be the better option. It's certainly better for my career than having a pool table or a dartboard up on the wall. It's still really hard to go to work in there, though. I do my weights, but the running machine makes my heart sink, which is why I prefer getting out of the house.

All the training I do these days is a far cry from the regimes we were given when I first started with Lancashire. Back in those days we would turn up for pre-season training at the end of March and have a net session in the sheds. Then we'd run to Chorlton baths and back, which is about two miles, and that was it. That was all we did to prepare for the season because the theory was that you got fit and stayed fit by playing. Things have changed a lot since then.

Getting fitter also helped me develop as a person. I feel a lot more confident about myself now than when I was a 25-stone walrus aged 20, that's for sure. I'm probably still not as fit as some of the people in the squad, but I have been known to win the fitness test competition, which the whole squad goes through before each tour. I won it before we went to the West Indies a couple of years ago and again before we went to India, so I can't be doing that badly. We do all sorts of different fitness challenges and the fact that I'm a contender for the title every now and then shows how far I've come since the bad old days. Fitness has become a part of my routine now and although it's still not something I particularly enjoy, I realise it's an important part of my life if I want to continue playing cricket at the highest level.

I've tried all sorts of different methods to help make training more enjoyable, sometimes training on my own, at other times working out with other people and even training as a team. Since Michael Vaughan became captain, there has been a lot more emphasis on fitness as a whole. I wouldn't say it changed anything for me because fitness was already a big part of my life, but it helped make us a successful team simply by working together. In the past it would be up to yourself when and where you went to the gym, but under Vaughan the team were encouraged to train as a unit. On one of the recent tours we were paired up with each other as gym buddies.

I'm not super-fit or anything like that but if I set out to do something, I believe it's very important to be confident that I can do it. That's where the motivation and determination come from.

When I'm training, I've always found that big statements don't work. There's no point setting yourself a target of doing this, that and the other three or four times a week when you know that more often than not you're not going to do it. Whenever I go to the gym I stop thinking about trying to do X, Y and Z because it doesn't work. I have a plan about what I want to do, but one that I can achieve. For instance, I would never say that for the next eight weeks I'm going to give up drinking, eat really healthily and train for four hours a day — that's hopeless because I'm never going to stick to it. You have to be realistic in what you're doing, otherwise you've got no chance.

Walking the walk — my route back to fitness before the Ashes involved a lot of walking and running around Rivington Pike near Bolton, mostly uphill. Dave 'Rooster' Roberts makes sure I don't slack, and we have a good laugh while we're training.

Rooster pushes me hard but I know it's for my own good.
He banishes me into his garage for some of the training!

Swimming is often used to warm down after a hard day in the field.

Rooster allowed no let up from the training routine during a few days break in Devon.

Bowling for the first time after recovering from another ankle problem.

FAMILY MAN

4

Home is a refuge from everything that goes on outside and, because I'm away such a lot, I regard time spent there with Rachael, Holly and Corey as precious.

As a professional cricketer I'm not able to spend as much time as I'd like at home, but I try to make the most of it when I am there.

One benefit of my job was avoiding all the chaos after we moved just after the Ashes series had finished. The removal vans had hardly unloaded before we travelled as a family to Australia for the Super Series. We came back via Dubai, where we had a short holiday, and were back no more than a couple of days before I had to leave for Pakistan. I had barely set foot in the new house since we moved in and did not arrive back until just before Christmas, by which time the place had been transformed. I don't think I'd have been much help with the unpacking and sorting out anyway, but Rachael had been very busy while I was away. I left it as a shell of a house, full of boxes, and got back to a home — it was great! It was just as well I thought so because I wouldn't have been brave enough to argue with Rachael over any of the details.

In our previous house I had a room where I threw all my junk until I needed it again. It was a bit like my corner of the dressing room, full of pads, bats, helmets and bags. In other words, it was a right tip. It soon became clear that I was unlikely to be given a similar room in our new house, so I've taken over the garage. All my gear is piled up in there until I need it again. I've never really understood garages anyway. You're meant to put your car in them but I don't know anybody who does — ours is already full of junk, encroaching on my kit. I think if we didn't have a garage, half the stuff would have been thrown out. Over the course of time I'd like to turn it into a wine cellar, but I'll have to get that past Rachael first.

Moving all my gear into the garage is not the only thing to have changed in my life since I met Rachael, got married and started a family. I used to have two friendly Boxer dogs, Arnold and Fred, but the busier I became the harder it was to look after them properly and take them for walks. My mum and dad started to help out more and more and a few years ago they moved in with my parents. The dogs are looked after very well and I get to see them when I visit. They still recognise me, especially Arnold, who spends most of his time playing with Holly. I don't really regard them as my dogs any more. I couldn't imagine taking them back now and I'm sure my mum and dad wouldn't part with them. They have an even better life now than they used to, ever since my parents moved to a semi-rural location where the dogs can run around to their hearts' content and play in the fields.

There was a time when the dogs and I spent a lot of time together and I miss taking them out for walks. It was good exercise for all of us. Once, Fred joined in with pre-season training at Lancashire, back in the days when that was not as intense as it is now. The squad was split into two groups for that particular day, and the lads who lived in the South Manchester area decided to do the session up near Glossop in Derbyshire. We planned to walk and do some running by the reservoir and I thought it would be a good idea to take Freddie with us. In those days he was an extremely boisterous dog — he's calmed down a lot now — and as soon as we started running he set off like a maniac. We had all sorts of trouble getting him back. I think we spent most of the time we were supposed to be training running after Freddie. By the time we'd caught up with him, we'd had enough and decided it would be a good idea to go to the pub and relax, which was the way things were done then. It wouldn't be approved of now, but if you think our group was bad, Ian Austin's lot spent their training day ten-pin bowling and playing pool!

One of the things I enjoy most about being at home is just relaxing and not doing very much. Rachael tends to take charge of the cooking if we're staying in to eat. I always offer, but she likes to do it so I don't argue. To be honest, we tend to eat out quite a lot. We enjoy going to restaurants as a treat. Mind you, I'm probably better than most people would expect in the kitchen. I left home at 16 years old when I first joined Lancashire, and lived in Chorlton, just up the road from Old Trafford, with a few of the lads. I had to learn how to cook then, and when I lodged with Pete Marron, the Old Trafford groundsman, in the grounds of Old Trafford, I had to look after myself. Believe it or not, we also had cooking lessons at the Academy in Australia, but that really wasn't for me. I volunteered to go out to Australia because I had not had the best of seasons and wanted to get better with bat and ball, not to learn how to cook a beef stroganoff. I'm not a useless cook by any means. I'm pretty confident that I could feed myself and others quite well, but I haven't cooked for about 18 months. I must confess that I haven't actually worked out how to use the cooker in our new house yet.

My diet is another thing that has had to change over the years. When I was younger and living in the centre of Manchester, it was a lot easier to go to one of the many take-away places near the flat than cook. Like most young lads, I enjoyed the social scene and that was part of it, but all that has changed now. Ever since I became really serious about my training and fitness I've also had to take a careful look at what I eat. From the moment I made the decision to get fitter I've had to count the calories. If you had met me in my local supermarket around that time, you would have seen me studying jars and packets to find out how many calories were in each item. These days I know what I can and cannot eat. I am aware of what I should and shouldn't be eating but I still eat a lot of stuff I probably shouldn't. I enjoy food and there are times when I let myself go a little bit and then I have to get myself back on track afterwards.

When I was on a rehabilitation programme early in 2006 after injuring my ankle, I was training hard and really had to watch what I ate. Ideally, if I ate something I shouldn't, I would be back in the gym the following morning trying to work it off, but that's not always the case. If I've been playing a lot of cricket or it's the end of a Test and I've had a few beers, I won't be that bothered about working them off. The worst food I eat these days tends to be when we take Holly out for a meal and I end up finishing her lunch!

Sadly, I haven't got the metabolism to burn off food naturally, so I have to work hard at it. Some players don't have the same problem. Jimmy Anderson, for instance, tries to put weight on but it just doesn't happen for him, no matter what he eats. It's the same with Paul Collingwood. He eats whatever he wants and doesn't put on any weight either. Unfortunately, I seem to put on weight just by looking at some food!

I love it when Rachael comes on tour with me, but we didn't think it would be a good idea for her to trail around Pakistan, heavily pregnant and with Holly in tow. There's no reason why all three of them can't come out to Australia and then on to the World Cup in the West Indies, though. It's great being an international cricketer and I'm very proud to play for England, but all these tours would turn into a prison sentence if I couldn't see Rachael and my family for months on end.

We made a conscious decision some years ago for them to travel with me as much as possible. That includes summer Test series at home. I don't think many people realise how much travel home series entail and it's not always easy living in a hotel for a week here and a week there with children. As we are in London a lot for Tests and functions we have now bought a flat down there as a base for Rachael and the kids when they come down with me. Back in the old days, even players who lived close to the ground would be expected to stay in the team hotel, but in the last few years those rules have been relaxed to allow the lads to spend more time with their families. So we stay together at the flat when I'm down in London for a Test, just like I stay at home when I'm playing in a Test at Old Trafford.

I'm sure having the family around helps me — it means I don't have to spend as much time with Steve Harmison for a start! I can come back to my room after a long day and switch off from whatever has been happening on the pitch. It doesn't matter how I've bowled or how many runs I've scored or whether we've won or lost, I still get the same reaction from my family and that's a great thing at any time.

Having that support from Rachael and the kids has made a massive difference to me. I don't think fatherhood has changed my outlook a great deal because having kids was something I always wanted and I really enjoy being a dad. I suppose the big difference is that your priorities change. Things that you once regarded as important seem less so when you become a dad. My kids and my family come before everything. Even the way I approach my cricket is different from the way it was before I had a family. I'm playing cricket now to provide for my family as well as to enjoy it. In the past I played for enjoyment and to get as far as I could in my career, but now I'm very conscious that what I do and how successful I am will also affect my family.

My desire to succeed has not diminished since I became a father. It's not made me any less determined to do well and I still want to perform. If I get out for a duck, I don't think, 'Oh well, there are more important things in life,' and head off home without a care in the world. If anything, having kids has made me even more determined to do well. I want my kids to be proud of me when they get older and I want to give them the best I can. The only way I can do that is by playing cricket well.

I love kids. I always knew I'd be a dad one day.

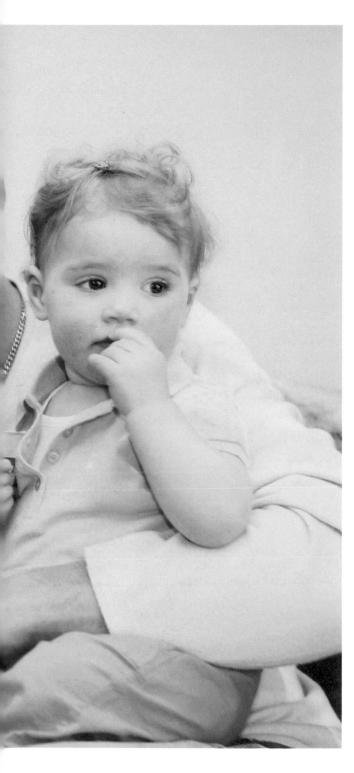

I want to give my kids the best — even if for Holly, at the moment, this means a soft green ball and a goldfish!

The garage is where I dump all my stuff — doesn't everybody?

AWAY FROM THE CROWD

5

Before we won the Ashes it was still reasonably easy to go out anywhere, but since then it's become a little more difficult. I can't go to many of the bars in and around Manchester any more because my face is too familiar. I'm a lot more self-conscious when I'm out now. Just going to the races or to watch Amir Khan's latest fight in Belfast became a big talking point. Suddenly everyone is interested in what I do and where I go, even if it's just for a drink in my local.

It was good to find some quiet time towards the end of our tour to India.

It's funny because all the things everyone seemed to quite like about me are suddenly regarded as a big problem. People have written that I'm very sociable and down-to-earth, yet suddenly by being sociable I'm doing something wrong. If people saw how hard I work in the gym and in the nets, I'm sure they would feel sorry for me. For instance, there was some criticism about me turning up at Ascot. What doesn't get reported is that I was up at 5.00 a.m. that day and put in four or five hours in the gym before I set off for the races. I could only go to Ascot because we were travelling in Paul Beck's helicopter, and the fact remains that I made sure I had done all my training beforehand. The problem is that people only see me out enjoying myself — they don't see me sweating like crazy at some unearthly hour trying to get fit for England.

In a three-month period in that summer of 2005, everyone seemed to get excited about five or six things I did but none of them was that outrageous. It's hardly rock 'n' roll, is it, going to Ascot races? Most of this sort of criticism just goes over my head. I'm happy with what I'm doing. If I'm honest, I'd sooner it didn't get written about, but it doesn't bother me that much. I have a fantastic family and I'm playing cricket for England, so I don't have that much to complain about. I'm certainly not about to apologise for getting out and about — there's nothing to apologise for.

I've got used to most of the media coverage, but some of it I still find over the top. For instance, when we went to a curry house in London one time I got a bit ratty with them. We'd booked a table and when we arrived there were paparazzi outside. The only people who could have tipped them off were the restaurant staff. I didn't blow my top or anything, but we left through the kitchens because the photographers were waiting outside all evening. I wouldn't have minded but it was the Saturday of the Lord's Test against Sri Lanka. They could have got as many pictures as they wanted on the field, but instead they waited all night outside a restaurant to get a picture of me with curry down my shirt.

If I do go out for a drink when I'm at home, I tend to go to a local bar that Michael Vaughan, the golfers Lee Westwood and Darren Clarke and I have a stake in. We are able to sit in a corner without being bothered. You often see a few well-known footballers in there because it's a bit of a safe haven, and I enjoy going there for the same reason. The bloke who runs it is a good friend of mine, knows all the old footballers and knows what he's doing. I don't go into Manchester very often these days but I've never been one for busy bars anyway. I was never really a nightclub man. I used to go in my younger days, but only to get a late drink. In those days the pubs used to close at eleven and I wasn't ready to go home then.

I'm more of a traditional pub sort of bloke. I did go to a nightclub-type place in London not long ago, which was apparently the in-place to be seen. I really didn't like it. It was fine one minute and suddenly around a thousand people suddenly turned up — it was horrific. I'd sooner go and have a quiet pint somewhere. There are some great pubs in London. It has become part of the England tradition to go out after The Oval Test at the end of the summer. Most of the lads head for the trendiest new bar, which is not usually my cup of tea. Steve Harmison and I go off in search of a proper pub and leave the rest of them to it. After the final Ashes Test a lot of them went looking for nightclubs, but I just stayed in the hotel bar and celebrated that way — as everyone saw the following day when I turned up a little worse for wear for the open-topped bus parade!

If I arrange to meet some mates, it will almost certainly be in a quiet pub rather than a major bar, so we can relax and enjoy ourselves. I'm very lucky because I have some good friends and while I'm bad at keeping in touch, it's good to see them when we do meet up. A classic example of that was when I came back from India and arranged to see a couple of the Lancashire lads in the pub and the whole team came out to have a few drinks. I still have friends in Preston, although the way my life is, I can go six or eight months without seeing some people, but as soon as I see them again I pick right up from where we left off last time. I know some people like to talk to each other day-in and day-out, and talk about very little, but I'm not like that. I just get on with it. I have my mates back in Preston and my mates where we live now. A couple of my old friends, both called Lee, even travelled out to the West Indies a few years ago when we were on tour, and it was good to hang out with them again. We managed to see quite a lot of each other because it was during the one-day series and it seemed to do nothing but rain for a couple of weeks.

I also spend quite a lot of time with Glen Chapple, Mark Chilton and my old team-mate Paddy McKeown, who is no longer on the staff at Old Trafford. Paddy is still one of my best mates. He was best man at my wedding and we go back a long way. I first met him when we were both coming through the age-group sides in Lancashire and we shared a flat for about five years, first in Preston and then at my flat at Castlefield, near Manchester. We were both on the staff at Lancashire then and probably enjoyed ourselves a little too much. We had some good times. We have just gone into business together, which is a good test of friendship if ever there was one. We run a hospitality company called Freddie and McKeown. It's very small scale as yet because I've got quite a lot of other things on the go, but it's good we are still team-mates.

Apart from the lads I grew up with at Lancashire, I suppose one of my biggest mates is Muttiah Muralitharan. Murali and I got friendly during his time at Lancashire and we've stayed in touch. We go for meals and chat about this and that. All he ever eats is crispy duck and a bucketful of rice when you go out with him, but he's good company. We struck up an almost immediate friendship from the moment he first breezed into the dressing room as Lancashire's overseas player back in 1999. When a new player arrives you always make an effort to make him feel at home. I found him amazing from the very first day. He is obviously an outstanding cricketer, which immediately earned the respect of the lads, but everyone liked him straight away anyway. He's excited about everything he does, which you don't find in everybody. It's almost as if he's playing cricket for the first time every time he picks up a ball. His great enthusiasm immediately rubbed off on me and all the rest of the lads in the Lancashire dressing room. It was hard not to like him, because of the way he is.

An example of just how popular he was with Lancashire was his leaving do a few years ago. Usually, a few of the lads will turn up and have a meal or a few drinks, but for Murali it was unbelievable. At the time we used to drink in a bar called Barca in the centre of Manchester and so many people wanted to come and wish him well that we had to hire a room there to fit everyone in. All the staff came, the people from the offices at Old Trafford, the players, the coaching staff, virtually everyone who was connected with Lancashire. They all turned up for Murali's leaving party, which is a good indication of how popular he was throughout the club. It's amazing when you think about it. He played for us for just three seasons, but in that short space of time he became incredibly popular. You could understand it if it was for someone like Wasim Akram, who played with us for about ten years, but to win over everyone in the club in such a short space of time shows that Murali is someone special. It also indicates how lucky we've been at Lancashire to have such tremendous overseas players, good fortune which has continued in the last few years with Brad Hodge and Andrew Symonds.

My other two closest friends are Neil Fairbrother and Chubby Chandler, who handle all my affairs and organise my days for me at International Sports Management. Neil took me under his wing when I was a young player at Lancashire and we've been close ever since. I speak to him a lot about my batting if I have a problem with that, and all sorts of other things. We probably talk two or three times a day and he gives me lots of advice about this, that and the other. I met Chubby, who owns ISM, through Neil and he has become an equally good friend. I've already mentioned how grateful I am for the mother of dressing-downs they gave me, which was the turning point in my career. The pair of them handle all my finances and investments and I'd be lost without them. If I need advice about anything, they are the first people I turn to after Rachael.

The people I tend to spend the most time with are, of course, the other players in the England squad. Playing with them so much, and being away from home together for most of the year, you're bound to develop strong friendships. Michael Vaughan encouraged a really strong team spirit on and off the pitch when he took over as captain, which has made it that much easier for me to step in on a temporary basis.

I got to know Vaughan for the first time back in 1998 when he was captain of the A tour we were on together, and we've become friends ever since. We have the same management company, and we socialise a lot away from cricket. Rob Key and Steve Harmison were also on the tour and the three of us became inseparable throughout that winter. I had met Harmison a few years earlier when I was captain of England Under-19s on tour in Pakistan and Steve was a raw and exciting young fast bowler. It has been well documented how Steve got homesick, and I spoke to him a lot before he went home to Ashington. The A tour management tried to split the three of us up because they thought we might form a clique, but it didn't have much effect on us because we still hung around together.

There are other members of the England team I've known for a long time. For instance I played with Marcus Trescothick in the junior age groups, so I've known him for many years, while all the seam bowlers are close. During his time as England's bowling coach, Troy Cooley, who has now gone back to do the same job with Australia, encouraged us all to spend time together and almost become a team within a team. I'm sure all the socialising helped us, especially when we won in the West Indies and South Africa, and definitely during the Ashes series.

I still spend plenty of time with Harmison. We always try for adjoining rooms on tour and just wander in and out of each other's pads. It helped both of us in Pakistan and India, because it can be very tough touring on the subcontinent. Steve brought his dartboard along and having a game soon became popular among the lads. I'm okay at darts, but not in the same league as Harmison and Hoggard, who were our stars of the oche out in India. Mind you, Steve is bound to be good because he's been playing at his local social club since he was about six! He and I opened up the connecting doors to our adjoining rooms and several of the lads would come around to throw some arrows for half an hour or so. Some of them, Geraint Jones for instance, got completely hooked on it — we couldn't get him out of the room. Alastair Cook was also keen and it was a nice way to get to know the new lads, in the room together playing darts and having a laugh. It was a great way of bonding we told Phil Neale, the tour manager, who sorts out our baggage. He was less than impressed because the dartboard wasn't just a simple affair. It came in a big case with a scoreboard and a pole to make sure the board was at the correct height, and an oche, and it weighed quite a bit. It kept being classed as excess baggage on flights. Phil was quite relieved when Harmison abandoned it before we came home. I think he feared that, because it was such a hit, it might become a permanent feature of England's touring kit.

Going to the Super Series during the winter taught me that you can't just build a team overnight, an important lesson. No matter how talented the individuals, you have to have some sort of team spirit if you are going to get through the tough times together and come out the other side. One of England's strengths during the last few years has been that we've all been together for some time and enjoy each other's company, on and off the pitch. This is in contrast to some of the sides I played in when I was younger. There was so much competition that some of your team-mates wouldn't even talk to you. I couldn't be doing with any of that and I've always gone out of my way to be friendly to anyone new who has come into the side — even if they are a threat to my place. It's a lot easier both socialising and playing with people you get on with. You don't see many teams that have a good team spirit struggling on the pitch.

Home is an oasis — being there gives me a chance to catch my breath and get up to date with life outside cricket.

Neil Fairbrother (left) and Chubby Chandler (right) are among
my closest friends as well as helping to organise my life.

Enjoying some 'down' time in India.

Whatever we're looking at, it isn't making us smile — or perhaps that's wedding-day nerves. My ushers flank brother Chris (on my left), the bridegroom, and best man Paddy McKeown (on my right).

I used to enjoy playing chess when I was at school, and was pleased to give Liam Plunkett a few games in India.

Taking an evening boat trip is a good way to unwind on tour. Matthew Hoggard, Gareth Batty and Jimmy Anderson thought so, too.

I'm not the tidiest person, as my hotel room in Mumbai demonstrates — typical of every other hotel room I've occupied when I'm away on tour really.

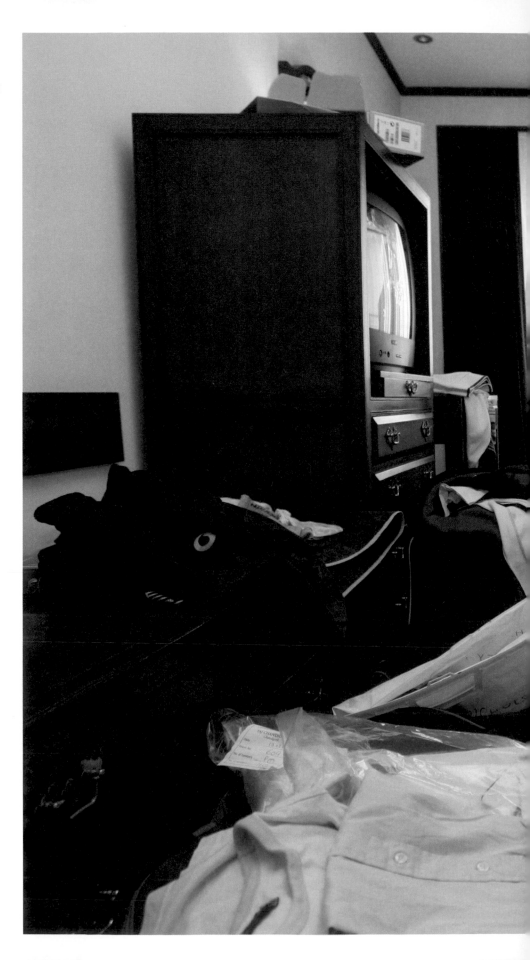

Steve Harmison's travelling dartboard became a popular part of the tour equipment in India. Most of the lads had a go. Steve was the best darts player in the squad — it must be all that time he spent playing darts in social clubs when he was younger.

Steve Harmison and I had adjoining rooms and everyone treated them as
a communal common room. Shaun Udal and the others often dropped by.

ROLE MODEL

6

The Ashes victory raised the profile of everyone who played in the series, so much so that a few of the lads were asked to endorse all sorts of products on the back of it. So far, I've resisted any offers to get involved in fashion shoots or clothes adverts. I have been offered the chance to model underwear, but can you imagine the stick I'd get at Lancashire and in the England dressing room if I did something like that? I'm not sure I'm confident enough about the way I look anyway. I'm a lot fitter than I used to be, but I don't really have a washboard stomach.

We had some fun while visiting the Magic Bus child development programme in Mumbai — high fives all round during the football game. We always try to visit a project for under-privileged kids while on tour.

I've never been one to follow fashion that closely anyway. Some members of the England dressing room think they are trendsetters, but I'd never claim to be one of them. I'd have to single out Jimmy Anderson and Kevin Pietersen as the ones with the most outrageous dress sense. They wear what they like and have the confidence to carry it off. I'm more middle of the road when it comes to the things I wear. I'm very much a polo-shirt with jeans sort of guy, and that's what I wear most of the time. I've never been one to browse in designer shops and I don't understand why some people would pay £300 for a shirt or a pair of trousers. That's just not me. I'd rather spend my money on other things, which is how I came to have a bit of a shopping spree when I was in India, because the clothes are so cheap. I like Lacoste tee-shirts, which are £70 or £80 at home, but in India are about £20 each. I presume they are the real thing and not fake, because I bought them from proper Lacoste shops. I left with polo-shirts in just about every colour they had — one for every day in the week.

I don't mind wearing suits. I need them because, as an England cricketer, I tend to go to quite a few benefit dinners and sponsors' functions and I can't turn out for Barclays Capital or Red Bull in tee-shirt and jeans. I bought four suits in India — hand-made for around £70 apiece. I used to spend a hell of a lot on clothes when I was younger. I suppose a lot of people are like that when they are young, but I've well and truly grown out of it. I hate shopping — I just can't stand it. If I had my way I'd order everything off the internet or mail order. Rachael often buys things for me, but I don't always like the things she picks out.

My only weakness when it comes to clothes is shirts. I like buying shirts, and the only shop I don't have to be dragged into is Mike Summerbee's. Mike got into the fashion business when he was still a Manchester City player and I've got to know him by going along to watch City. I buy most of my shirts from him now. It's very easy for me. He measures me up, I choose the styles or colours and he delivers them. It's simple and it means I don't have to drag around any other shops.

I may not be very interested in keeping up with the latest fashion, but I am careful to make sure that whatever I agree to endorse is a product that I really like and use. I have a contract with Woodworm for instance because I use their bats. Another of the contracts I have is with the energy drink Red Bull. I do drink it myself, so it's not as though I'm going around advertising something I wouldn't pour down my own throat. All my sponsorship deals have developed over a long period of time and that's why I like them. I'm involved with Volkswagen because they have a good relationship with ISM, who look after my affairs, and with Thwaites because it's a northern brewery and they have been associated with Old Trafford for many years.

The big problem with endorsing anything is that people understandably want you to help out for a day here and a day there and I can allocate only so much time to that. It's important to set time aside for the family and to practise and train. If I let that slip and my game deteriorated, there is a good chance most of these sponsors would stop being interested in me anyway. Neil Fairbrother and I consult the diary to see what I've got on, and only then can we start promising to do other things. If I sign up for an endorsement, I want to give the people as much time as I can, and good time at that, rather than five minutes here and ten minutes there. I'm very happy with what I'm doing at present and with what I earn. I suppose I could bring in a lot more for my family by spreading myself much more thinly, but I'd rather develop good relationships with a few people than fizz about from one thing to another.

Perhaps the best part about becoming better known after the Ashes is that I can use my name to help others and help good causes. That is particularly the case in my benefit year, during which we are hoping to raise a million pounds for charity. I was impressed at how David and Victoria Beckham raised money through an auction at their pre-World Cup party and I'd like to use my name in a similar way. After my benefit year is over I intend to set up a foundation with Paul Beck, Lancashire's main sponsor and the chairman of my Benefit Committee, to raise more money for charity on an annual basis. The idea is to have several functions a year — golf days or dinners or something along those lines — and the proceeds would go to various children's charities.

It's great to be able to do something like this. You only have to look at Ian Botham to see what can be done. I think he has raised more than £10 million for charity over the years, and something like £300 million indirectly. It all started when he visited a leukaemia ward and it touched him so much he wanted to do something about it. Since he's been involved with the charity, some amazing work has been done. Before he started raising money, leukaemia sufferers had a 20 per cent chance of survival, but with all the money Botham has brought in research has progressed and there is now an 80 per cent chance of surviving. When Ian gets home at night and relaxes in his armchair, he should feel very proud of what he's achieved. He's made a huge difference to a lot of people's lives. I would love to be able to do something similar.

There are lots of deserving charities, of course, but those involving children are close to my heart. I've got kids of my own and I've always enjoyed being around children, so it's only natural I should want to help them out. When you go to some of the places I've visited, such as the Francis House Children's Hospice in Manchester, it is impossible not to be moved. When we are on tour these days, in Bangladesh, say, or India, several members of the England squad will take the time to visit sick children or an orphanage. You'd be amazed what a buzz the kids get out of this. They love the fact that some England cricketers have turned up. Quite often we will organise a game of Kwik Cricket with them and it's great to see how fast some of them pick it up, even those who have never played before.

I don't have any long-term ambitions to coach but I do like coaching kids — for fun rather than getting technical with them. I like the kids to have a laugh while they're playing, rather than teaching them how to play a forward defensive shot. In my opinion, kids should just go out and play the game and not be restricted by people telling them what they can and can't do. When I was between nine and twelve, I had a really nice bowling action. I used to bowl chest-on and swung the ball away, but once the staff coaches employed by England got hold of me, they changed it all. I remember them saying to me that I'd never bowl out-swing like that and trying to get me to bowl side-on. I'm sure that was partly to blame for me hurting my back.

Now whenever I coach kids, I tell a quick bowler to bowl as fast as he can and not worry about anything else. One of the hardest things to do on a cricket field is bowl fast. If you find someone who can do it, why bother them with trying to coach the right action or making sure their head is in the right place? It's the same if you find one of the young kids who can spin the ball — I just tell them to spin it as hard as they can. If a batsman can hit the ball, let him hit it as hard as he can. It's important cricket is kept simple, especially for young kids. The thing that used to frustrate me when I was starting out was when they used to stop the game to tell you where you were going wrong instead of letting you get on with it. The big thing for kids when they are playing cricket is that they enjoy it.

Always a pleasure to give Shane Warne advice, even when I'm not playing — standing as umpire in Liam Botham's benefit match at Southampton.

Visiting hospitals in the UK is on the agenda as often as possible — this one is in Guildford in Surrey.

Ian Botham came up on stage at one of my benefit dinners. Beefy can be very proud of himself after raising so much money for charity.

Shaun Udal and I with the Magic Bus kids in Mumbai.

OTHER SPORTING WORLDS

7

Like most professional sportsmen, I have an interest in sports other than my own. I go to watch Manchester City's games every now and then but I wouldn't call myself as big a football fan as, for instance, Steve Harmison, who goes to watch Newcastle United every chance he gets. I enjoy the social side of watching City. Paul Beck has a box there and it's good to be able to hang out and watch the matches with friends. I was even presented with a shirt and taken out on to the pitch to wave to the fans after we won the Ashes. Who says football fans have no time for cricket?

Horse racing is a different world — and now I'm an owner myself I take an extra interest in it.

One of my favourite sports outside cricket is boxing. I first got into boxing a couple of years ago when I trained at a gym in Salford to help with my fitness prior to the tour to South Africa. I still follow it from a safe distance. As part of Sky's coverage of the cricket in 2006, they asked me to contribute to their *Cricket AM* programme by trying my hand at different sports. I played darts with Phil 'The Power' Taylor, tried rugby goal-kicking with Charlie Hodgson and challenged Stuart Pearce to a penalty-taking competition. One of the most testing assignments was going over to Ricky Hatton's gym to spar with him in the ring. Ricky 'The Hitman' Hatton is a welterweight and I've known him on and off for seven or eight years. He's really good company. He's also very good at what he does.

I went down to the gym where he trains to watch him work out and I was supposed to hold up pads while he practised hitting them. That wasn't too bad, but then they wanted me to put on a body-bag and get in the ring with him. As soon as I got in, Ricky told me to stand on the ropes and not in the middle because otherwise he'd knock me into them. I wasn't arguing. I was too busy wondering whether this was such a good idea. The transformation in Ricky was incredible. One minute he was chatting to me quite normally, the next he had become this mad punching machine, and he was coming at me like a Rottweiler. He was so fast, he was all over me. As it happened, it didn't hurt, although I could feel the punches through the body-bag. I'm just glad I had that protection because otherwise I'd have come out of the ring with all my ribs broken, and I can imagine what England would have said about that!

It was a great experience and makes you realise how good these guys are when you see them in action from close range. I also enjoyed the chat we had afterwards. Ricky was talking about the things he has done to improve by just one or two per cent, which is often the difference between winning and losing at the top level. Everything boxers do outside the ring is designed to prepare them for what it will be like in the ring. Preparation is the key. They build up their stamina, their strength and all the moves through drills and circuits, sparring and pad-work — and everything they do from week to week gets harder and harder.

Going into the ring and sparring is probably the hardest thing I've ever done. It's all right just standing there and punching, but when you've got to think about moving around to avoid the other guy's punches, you get very tired, very quickly. I've got a speed-ball in my own gym, but nothing prepares you for quite how tiring it is when you get into the ring. I did think about getting a punch-bag, but the problem with that is you need someone standing behind it when you're punching. I was also scared the ceiling might come through if I put one up, and I don't think Rachael would be too impressed if that happened.

Another of the sports I enjoy is darts, although I wasn't very successful when I played against Phil 'The Power' Taylor for the Sky programme. I do enjoy watching it. I wanted to go to the world championships, which are held over the New Year period, but it perhaps wouldn't have been the best idea just before the tour to India. I did wonder about going in disguise, with a false beard and a wig or something, but if I had been discovered it could have got very messy with a load of drunken darts fans! Instead, a few of us watched the afternoon session in one of the Manchester bars, went and had a bit of tea and then came back for the evening session — it was a great day.

Other than cricket, though, I suppose horse racing is my favourite sport. I find it very relaxing and enjoy the social side of things. It has become even more enjoyable since I became part-owner of a horse. It's called Flintoff, so it's pretty obvious it's connected to me, but I didn't name it. Paul Beck bought the horse a few years ago and I got a phone call from his little lad, James, who was about five at the time. He told me his dad had bought a horse and he was allowed to name it and asked me if I minded him calling it Flintoff. Of course, I had to say fine, not thinking I would have anything to do with it other than going to watch it run a couple of times. So it came as a big surprise when Paul gave Rachael and me half the horse as a wedding present, which was very generous of him, but I must admit I'd have liked to re-name it. It's a bit embarrassing going to the races and everyone knowing that it's your horse. I've also been landed with half the training fees — you get half of everything when you became a half-owner!

The horse has done very well for us. He's won five out of seven races — a decent horse is Flintoff. We got him as a four-year-old and in 2005 he ran in some flat races for young horses and then went over the hurdles. He's not run for a while because he ran quite a lot of hard races on firm ground and developed a problem with the back of his ankle. If he'd carried on running, it could have become serious, but he's young enough to come back after a rest. When I was told about his troubles, they sounded very familiar. Maybe he has got the right name after all!

What I like about going racing is that it's completely different from what I'm used to. I know what Sir Alex Ferguson means by saying he finds racing a good way to get away from the day job, because that's exactly the way I feel about it. I'm not a gambler by any means, but I'll have a fiver or a tenner here or there. I don't attract much attention at the races, either. I get asked to sign the odd thing but most of the people are there to watch the racing.

Ascot was just a bit much for me. I had to wear a top hat and tails, but I'm not Fred Astaire, I'd sooner go in a tee-shirt and jeans to a smaller meeting where I can relax and enjoy myself rather than be on parade.

Since I became an owner I have started to follow the sport a bit more. I look out for Paul's horses, and other horses I've heard of, but I don't know that much about the sport, which is how I like it. I don't want to be totally wrapped up in it. I just like to go and watch. If I know a horse is running I might buy the *Racing Post* and have a little flutter, but I'm not a big punter or one of these people who can tell you about every race and every horse's form. A few of the lads ask me for tips but I'm always a bit wary about that in case anything goes wrong. I remember we were playing a one-day international at Headingley a couple of years ago and I'd been told to look out for a particular horse. I told all the lads and someone was sent out to put on a load of bets. Of course, it never came close to coming in and I got plenty of stick about that, so I've been a bit reluctant to pass on any more tips since then.

I started to watch rugby union a few years ago when we were on tour in Sri Lanka while the rugby World Cup was on in Australia. Each time England played, we'd all gather to watch in one of the bars and it was great to see them lift the trophy by beating Australia in the final. We used to get really up for the matches and watching Jonny Wilkinson put that winning kick over with seconds to go was fantastic. Everyone in the bar jumped up and started celebrating. I still like watching England and I've been to Twickenham to watch the odd game, but because I'm away a lot I don't get as much chance to support them as I'd like.

The sport I love most, of course, is cricket. It's been a huge part of my life from as far back as I can remember. From my very earliest days growing up in Preston, I was surrounded by it. My dad, Colin, played most of the weekend and my mum, Susan, took my brother Chris and me along to watch. Given that background, it's hardly surprising I ended up doing what I do now. My childhood gave me a great love of the game, which is still with me. All the time I've spent playing since, and the time I've spent practising and training, has all been worthwhile. Many times I'd rather be doing something other than training, and there have been times when I've actually disliked the game, but that feeling doesn't last long.

On several occasions, everything has seemed to be stacked against me, but I suppose all players go through that at some stage and I've never got to the point when I've fallen out of love with the game. I'm in the fortunate position of being able to earn a good living from cricket and, in some ways, I'm probably living my dad's dream because I'm sure he'd have loved to have been a professional cricketer. He helped to give me every opportunity when I was younger and, having reached the level I now have, I feel I'm playing for him and the rest of my family every time I go out on to the field. Cricket is something I love doing, but it's also very important because it gives my family a good quality of life.

Some days, especially when I'm bowling, I'm sore and hurting and not looking forward to going out there to play, but those days are few and far between. Most days I love getting out there and doing my best. I feel very comfortable on that particular stage. When I play cricket I don't have any inhibitions and I'm confident in what I'm doing, which is not always the case in other aspects of life. In a social situation when I don't know many people, for instance, I'm not the confident bloke people see taking catches at slip or batting and bowling. Out in the middle, I'm confronting situations that I've come across time and again. It's like going to the office. I've played cricket for nearly 20 years now, at one level or another, and I'm at ease doing it and playing in front of a crowd. I've made sacrifices along the way, probably not as many as I should have done early in my career, but I still like to go out and have a beer every now and then. I suppose the secret to success is finding that balance, so you can still perform consistently for England, and I hope I've cracked that now.

There are times when the cricket is tough going. The winter tour to Pakistan is one example. I don't know whether it was because it was at the back end of a long summer or the first time I'd toured without the family, but I found Pakistan a tough trip. Yet just a few weeks later, I was really enjoying India. I can't ever see me getting to the stage when I don't enjoy cricket. I believe careers are going to get shorter with the amount of cricket we are playing. When you talk to retired players, they always say your playing days are the best days of your life so I really want to make the most of what time I've got left as a player. Some people — Phil DeFreitas springs to mind — play on and on. I think he was nearly 40 by the time he packed up, but even if I wanted to carry on that long, I'm not sure my body would allow it.

I've not really thought about how long I want to carry on playing. I'm doing a little work with Sky television now, which is giving me a bit of experience in front of the camera. I enjoy doing that, so maybe that is an avenue I could explore in the future, but you don't know what's going to happen in a few years' time. Some people have suggested I might play on in county cricket after my time with England is up, but if I can still play, I think I'll want to carry on playing international cricket. Then again, I do enjoy playing for Lancashire. It's been a long-term ambition of mine to become captain of Lancashire, but whether that opportunity will ever arise I don't know. At this stage of my career, I can't make firm plans that far ahead. I'll keep my options open and see what happens when the time comes.

Golf is not my game, but I hack my way round a course every now and then.

Having a go at other sports for Sky's *Cricket AM* was an interesting experience. Bowling — the ten-pin variety — wasn't too bad.

I'm not a real gambler but find racing's social side enjoyable. Since most people are there to watch the horses, I don't attract much attention and can relax.

Charlie Hodgson of Sale Sharks instructed me in the art of kicking the rugby ball.

Although I've known Ricky Hatton for some time, it was a revelation when I got into the ring with him — an experience I'd rather not repeat.

ON AND OFF
THE FIELD

8

In 2006, when it became clear Michael Vaughan
was not going to be fit for the start of the summer,
the selectors re-appointed me as stand-in captain
for the three-Test series against Sri Lanka. Just as
in India, plenty was said and written about whether
the captaincy would be too much for me to handle
on top of being an all-rounder. In fact, I think I was
a better captain by the time the Sri Lankan series
started, simply because I had the experience of
leading the side in India, although you wouldn't have
thought so, judging by what was written after the
First Test at Lord's.

Attending the Beckham's pre-World Cup party was an unexpected pleasure,
and a great night.

I bowled more than 70 overs. I thought that was the best choice, given the context of the game. A few decisions I made were criticised. For instance, I didn't bowl the spinner as much as people thought I should have done, but Liam Plunkett beat the bat about 30 times. While the seamers were doing well, I wanted to keep them going. The conditions were perfect for seam bowling, the batsmen were playing and missing — and we dropped ten catches. We took 29 wickets in the game and at the end of it my captaincy came into question! It was the dropped catches that cost us the win, not my captaincy. If we had held our catches, we could have won halfway through Saturday, but instead we were still trying to bowl them out on Monday evening. One thing that perhaps gave a false impression of the wicket was Sajid Mahmood taking three quick wickets in the first innings with fast in-swinging yorkers. That enabled us to enforce the follow-on, but it wasn't that bad a wicket and they battled hard to survive for a draw.

After the experience of Lord's, we moved on to Edgbaston, where I began to realise that luck plays a big part in whether you're regarded as a good or bad captain. Everything seemed to go right for me at Edgbaston. I took myself off after two overs of the first innings, brought Plunkett on and he took two wickets in his first over. I moved a fielder from midwicket to fourth slip and the next ball was edged straight there. Everything happened virtually straight away, but I could just as easily have been made to look a fool — it's a fine line between success and failure. There will be days when I try things and nothing works and others when everything works. You can't control how a bowler bowls or a batter bats. All you can do is try to make the bowling changes at the right times and put the fielders where you think they should go. A lot of it is guess-work. At least this time we came away with a victory by six wickets and were aiming to wrap up the series at Trent Bridge.

We started the next Test brightly as well and had Sri Lanka reeling on 169 for 9 until Murali came out swinging his bat. We had been doing so well and he came out smiling as usual and swinging at everything. What can you do in a situation like that? You try to put fielders in the right places but you just can't budget for someone like that. I was tearing my hair out in frustration. He's my big mate and I'm as desperate to get him out as anyone, but he hit 33 runs and added 62 for the final wicket, which proved crucial to the balance of the match.

One thing that disappointed me about that Test was that we were playing in England and could just as well have been in Colombo from the condition of the pitch. When we turned up and looked at the Trent Bridge wicket it was obvious that it was going to break up and turn square — just what you want with Murali in the opposition!

If you're taking on Sri Lanka and Murali, you want to face them on a fast, bouncy wicket that's going to fly through or, failing that, a green-top that is going to nibble around. I'm not making any excuses, but bowlers who bang it into the wicket like I do were pretty ineffective on it. Monty Panesar, England's only spinner, bowled well and got five wickets, but with all respect to Monty, he's not a Murali. Their lads really struggled against Monty, so when we faced Murali it was always going to be a tough task. Having said that, we probably lost the Test when we failed to get a first-innings lead. However many we had to chase in the second innings would be extremely tricky against Murali, so if we didn't get a decent lead we knew we'd be struggling, and we lost by 134 runs.

Throughout that Test I was feeling my left ankle again. I had felt a niggle at Edgbaston and it got worse during Trent Bridge. It's happened before in my career. I seem to have a period of rest, play for a while and then get a sore ankle again. After the Test I had scans and X-rays and they found inflammation from the operation I had on my ankle after coming back from South Africa at the start of 2005, and some tiny bone fragments. I was 16 stone during the Test series against Sri Lanka and there was eight times my body-weight going through my front foot, so to put my ankle problems down to three minute fragments took some swallowing.

There was all sorts of talk about having another operation to take them out, but two specialists couldn't guarantee the fragments were causing the problem, so that didn't seem a good enough reason to operate. Instead, I had over a month off and spent six or seven hours a day with Rooster Roberts doing a lot of work to strengthen my ankle with different exercises. Everyone kept talking about how important it was that I was fit for the Ashes in the winter of 2006, but I was looking beyond that. I was thinking about the rest of my career. Everyone seemed to be transfixed by the five-month period, covering the Ashes and the World Cup, but after that five months my career isn't going to stop. I want to carry on playing cricket for the next four of five years. Every bowler has an area of weakness and my ankle is mine, but I have got to do everything I can to make sure I can prolong my career for as many years as possible.

The ankle injury and the defeat at Trent Bridge left me frustrated and disappointed, but I still enjoyed leading the side and it has not put me off captaincy. I probably have a few more doubters about my ability to do it now than I did after we won the Test in Mumbai, but I'd like to do it again, if given the opportunity. One thing I really noticed during my time as captain against Sri Lanka was a definite change in the way the press reacted to me. Maybe it's because there are more of them about for home Tests than when we're abroad, but there is a definite change if you lose at home.

When you win and you're doing all right, the interviews you do afterwards with Sky and Channel Five are all nicey-nicey, but when you get beaten it's totally different. I noticed it in particular in the press conference at Trent Bridge. The atmosphere had changed and journalists wouldn't make eye contact, they just asked questions. Normally, I have a bit of chit-chat with various members of the press, but there was none of that before or after the press conference this time. It was a lot less amiable than usual. I don't expect pats on the back when we lose, but the difference was very noticeable.

There was a lot of talk about my activities away from the pitch, too, particularly before the Second Test. I went over to Belfast on the Saturday night to watch Amir Khan's latest fight, returning by helicopter the following morning because I was due to start the Great Manchester 10 kilometre Run, and then Rachael and I went to a party given by David and Victoria Beckham in the evening. If I had just gone out socialising around home, no one would have been any the wiser, but helicopters are a bit high-profile. It's not something within my regular travel budget. Maybe I should look for a helicopter company to sponsor me? Until I find one, Paul Beck was good enough to lay it on so that I could be back to do my stuff in Manchester by 10.00 a.m. Even then, I only just made it to the starter's rostrum.

We got back in time, but I didn't allow for crowds going into Manchester to watch the race. I got stuck in a traffic jam, crawled right up to some bollards that stopped cars from going any farther, and had to get out to explain the situation to a steward. I was starting the race I told him, and could he please move the bollards. He was a bit suspicious about this story and asked me who I was. Eventually a policeman came along and gave me a police escort to about 200 yards from the start-line. It was absolutely pouring down with rain that day and I had to make an embarrassed dash to the start, wearing my big boots and jeans, so I could make it in time.

Anyway, we won the Second Test, which answers those who feared I might be burning the candle at both ends. I do have one regret, though. I was lucky enough to be invited to Frankfurt by the BBC to watch England's opening match against Paraguay in the World Cup. It was a great experience. Some 60,000 England fans were cheering the team on. We had lunch and afterwards the BBC asked me to do an interview. I thought I'd done a great interview about how much I wanted England to do well and go far in the Cup. I was really enthusiastic, but when the phones started to ring and the text messages came in, I gathered some people thought otherwise. Apparently, my tongue got a bit carried away and I didn't make a lot of sense, which, sadly, I have to blame on a very good lunch topping up the alcohol from a friend's birthday party the night before. They had a good laugh in the dressing room, but I was disappointed with myself because I try to be a good role model for kids and at that time a lot of them would have been watching.

Getting to watch England in the World Cup is one of many opportunities that have come my way since we won the Ashes. I've also met many people I'm sure I wouldn't have met otherwise. It's very strange because when you become well known and you meet someone else who is well known, no one ever introduces themselves. It's almost like a secret code. Everyone expects other people to know who they are, so they don't greet each other like normal people do in everyday life. I've found all that side of things a bit strange, but I don't tend to get very starstruck anyway. I suppose if I really thought about the people I was meeting I might, but they are just people at the end of the day. The only time I got really starstruck was in my early days when I first walked into the Lancashire dressing room and found Neil Fairbrother, Michael Atherton and Wasim Akram in there. That was really frightening — sharing a dressing-room with some of your heroes.

The various events arranged for my benefit year, have given me the chance to meet Alan Shearer and Gabby Logan, and find out how people from different sports train and perform.

One of my daydreams is to have a walk-on part in the TV series *Shameless*. I'm a big fan of the programme and several of the lads, particularly Steve Harmison and me, watched it religiously while we were in Pakistan. I met David Threlfall, who is the producer of the programme and also stars as the main character, Frank Gallagher, at the Angel Ball. This was a big event to raise funds for Kirsty Howard, a little girl who fronts the campaign for the Francis House Children's Hospice in Manchester. I met David again at a match at Maine Road and invited him into our box for a chat about this and that. I think he did actually write me into one of the episodes, which would have been great. Don't get me wrong, I'm not one of these sports stars who fancies themselves as an actor when they retire, but being in *Shameless* was something I would have loved to have done. Unfortunately, the filming was in October, just before I was due to go to Pakistan, so it never happened.

David did promise to come to one of my benefit events, though. We had a dinner at Old Trafford football ground and after the meal there was the usual question-and-answer session with James Nesbitt grilling me, Sir Alex Ferguson, Bryan Robson and Michael Vaughan. Right in the middle of this, David Threlfall staggers through the audience in his Frank Gallagher role. For those who don't follow *Shameless*, he plays a down-and-out with long greasy hair and a green parka, who is almost permanently drunk. He walked right up to the stage, interrupted the question-and-answer session and did a ten-minute stand-up routine during which he opened his coat to reveal a Manchester City shirt, much to the amusement of Sir Alex Ferguson. Michael Vaughan didn't know what was going on. He thought some drunk had gatecrashed and couldn't understand why no one was doing anything about getting him off the stage.

Another of the big highlights of my benefit year was a concert given by Elton John at a special dinner at Battersea Park. Unfortunately, I may have ruined it for the guests because I got on stage to sing with him. Apart from that, it was a fantastic night for everyone who was there. We started off with a question-and-answer session with Darren Gough and me, and former England rugby union captains Martin Johnson and Lawrence Dallaglio, which went down well, and then the main event came on. All the time I knew the moment would come when I'd have to get up on that stage and join Elton. He played a couple of songs and I was fine but halfway through the third one I started to get nervous because I knew 'Rocket Man' was next. This was the song I was supposed to sing. There was no chance of refusing at my own benefit dinner, was there? I've got used to performing in front of big crowds for England as a cricketer, but this was something else. England team karaoke nights had nothing on this.

Elton called me up on stage and I stood there propping up the piano, loosened my tie and my top button, like I'd seen all the singers do, and tried to do a bit of crooning. As I was singing, I was looking out at people I knew who were just loving seeing me squirming with embarrassment, but I loosened up after a minute or two and played up a bit to those nearest the stage. I made sure I sang very low, so you could hardly hear me under Elton's voice, which is so strong. He did look after me, singing just a bit louder when we duetted to try to drown me out a little. It was a surreal night all round. At dinner I was sitting next to Elton John, whose records I'd grown up listening to, chatting about cricket and all different kinds of things. It was an amazingly generous gesture on his part to come along. We didn't pay him anything. He just turned up, was absolutely brilliant and rocked the whole place.

As if that experience wasn't enough, out of the blue Rachael and I also received an invitation to attend the Beckhams' party, which was held shortly before the England football team set off for Germany and the World Cup. I didn't know quite what to expect, but once we got there it was great. All the England football squad were there. The only one I'd met before was Gary Neville, whom I knew from playing cricket with his brother Phil, but I hadn't seen him in years. You hear all these things about footballers but they just seemed great lads who are exceptionally good at what they do. They reminded me a lot of the England cricket squad. They all seemed to get on well together and had a good spirit among themselves, which was great to see.

David and Victoria made us feel really welcome. They were excellent hosts. What people also forget is that they raised £1.5 million for charity at the auction that night. Not many people can do that. They are using the position they are in for the greater good. The entertainment was fabulous too. We had Robbie Williams and James Brown singing for us — how good is that? I was chuffed to be invited in the first place, but how many people would turn down the chance of seeing James Brown live? I wasn't asked to go up on stage this time, but I was waiting and primed if asked!

Nasser Hussain, Michael
Atherton and David Gower
came over to chat after
my first day as England
captain in Nagpur.

Left: Tossing the coin at Lord's, my first home Test as England captain. Leading the side out there was a special experience.

Above: Sajid Mahmood made his Test debut at Lord's, and I was delighted to hand him his England cap.

My captaincy at Lord's was criticised, but I wouldn't do much different if we played the game again.

If we'd held our catches at Lord's, we'd have won the
Test easily, but instead Sri Lanka fought back for a draw.

Above: We finished the right side of that fine line in the Second Test
— to Alastair Cook's delight as well as mine.

Right: Everything that went wrong at Lord's went right at Edgbaston.
Liam Plunkett bowled just as well in the previous Test but it was in
the second one that he got some deserved reward.

Left: Kevin Pietersen's successive centuries at Lord's and Edgbaston were special innings from a special player.

Bottom: I bowled a lot of overs in the three Tests against Sri Lanka, but it was what was needed in each match.

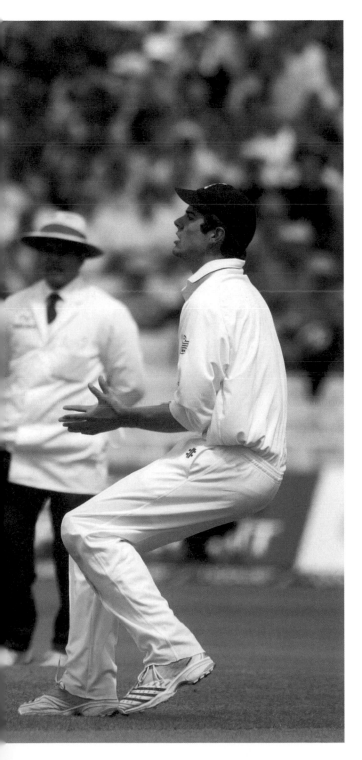

Left: After all those catches were dropped at Lord's, I wanted to make sure I caught this one at Edgbaston.

Above: Walking off the field with my old mate Muttiah Muralitharan after we had won the Edgbaston Test.

Murali put in another match-winning performance at Trent Bridge. He took the game away from us with the bat and then bowled us out on a responsive pitch.

Another problem with my left ankle meant I missed the
rest of the season after the Test series against Sri Lanka.

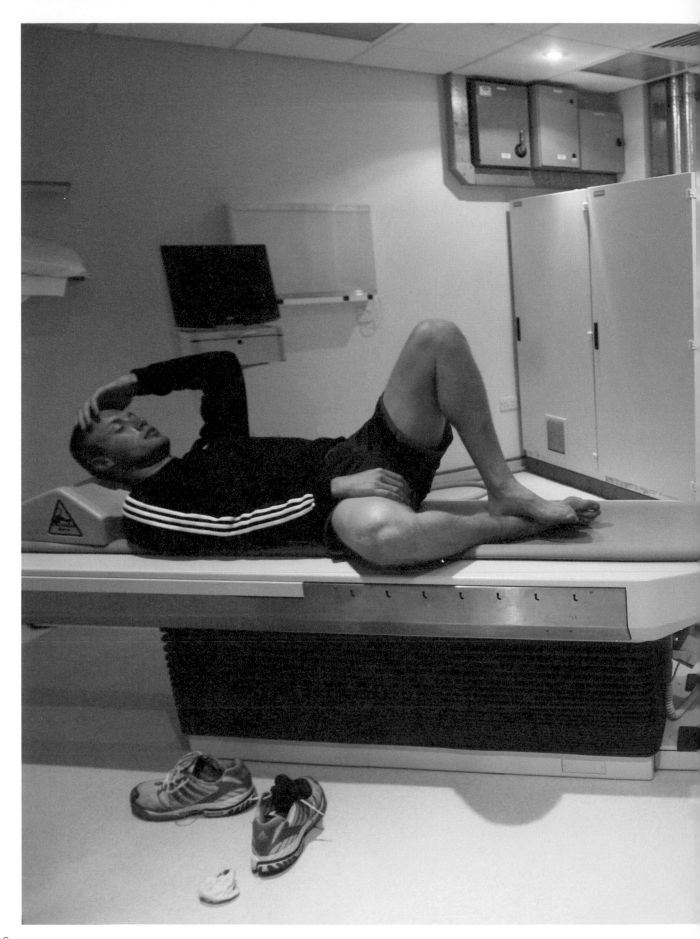

Preparing to undergo the scan that confirmed my ankle problems were not over and I would be out for the rest of the season.

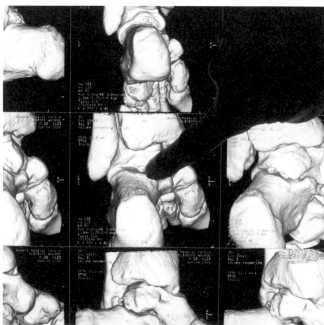

Right: Before starting rehabilitation for my ankle, Steve Harmison and I joined
Alan Ball to watch England play their opening match of the World Cup in Frankfurt.

During my benefit year, I found myself in company with a few people I may not otherwise have met, David Threlfall and James Nesbitt (left) for instance. They both attended a dinner at Old Trafford football ground, as did Sir Alex Ferguson and Bryan Robson (right).

Media interest has increased a lot since the Ashes, particularly for me, as captain, in India

MY KIND
OF MUSIC

9

As well as sport, which has been a massive part of my life from an early age, another big interest of mine is listening to music. I used to work on the record counter — they still had records and not CDs in those days — at Woolworths in Preston. That was after I'd first signed on as a professional at Lancashire, and ever since then I've been a music fan.

Singing with Elton John was a big highlight for me — although I'm not sure the crowd that night would agree.

Working in the record department introduced me to a wide range of music — not just the stuff that was in the charts around that time. We played everything, from the latest releases to Elvis Presley and Frank Sinatra. I listen to music all the time in the car, and in the dressing room, so it's ever-present in my daily activities. The only place I don't listen to it much is at home, but that's because I'm too busy. It's hard to think what I do at home, but time just seems to fly by.

Rachael and I have very different tastes in music and let's just say that I struggle with what she listens to. James Blunt is not my thing at all. She's also into Debbie Harry at the moment and seems to listen to her non-stop. I prefer to listen to Radio Two in the car and when Rachael tries to put one of her CDs on, I tell her she has until the count of five to take it out or it goes out of the window. I think Steve Harmison was amazed when we gave him a lift somewhere once because there were all these CDs flying out of the window. I think we got through a couple of mine and a couple of hers before we settled on something we both liked.

I don't follow the charts and wouldn't be able to tell you who is in the Top Ten at any given time, but I can tell you that a right load of dross gets played in the England dressing room. Some of it is absolutely terrible, but that might be a sign that I'm getting old! I think the last few years must have caught up with me because I just can't see why anyone would like some of that R'n'B music. They listen to artists such as 50 Cent. All it does for me is give me a headache. If I had my way and was to bring in a CD compilation of all my favourite tracks, it would be filled with Elvis Presley, Frank Sinatra, Rod Stewart, Elton John and perhaps a bit of Johnny Cash. I'd also include Dean Martin and the crooners. That music doesn't really go down well in the dressing room, but since I have stood in as captain they haven't had any choice because I've been in charge. I like to think I've gone some way towards educating some of them into what good music should sound like, although some members of the dressing room are lost causes. Kevin Pietersen is beyond hope when it comes to musical taste. He's very much in the 50 Cent camp.

As much as I like music, I've never claimed to be a very good singer. Anyone who was in Trafalgar Square after the Ashes and heard my attempt at singing 'Suspicious Minds' would testify to that. The same could be said of my attempt to duet with Elton John, but fortunately he drowned me out. A very strange story circulated after the Ashes that I was going to have singing lessons and start releasing records. All I can say is that the world is very lucky that story wasn't true. I think it all stemmed from a fiftieth birthday party I went to at Old Trafford for Pete Marron, Lancashire's groundsman. A band was playing and it ended up as a karaoke night. Someone took a picture of me singing on stage and it got in one of the papers the following day. Next thing I know I was being approached by some music company asking me if I'd like to record something. How desperate could they get?

Some of the lads use music as a pick-up to inspire them before going out on to the field, but I don't get fired up by hearing a good song on the iPod. I'm not the sort of player to go out on to the pitch so pumped up with adrenalin that my eyes are bulging out of my head and I start getting aggressive and fiery. What the right record can do is put a spring in my step. Sitting in a quiet dressing room with nothing going on can get quite boring, but when you put some music on it often sparks an atmosphere.

The great example of that was during our Test win in Mumbai over the winter. It was an important Test for us and I'd spoken a hell of a lot to the team about various things as we tried to win it and level the series. Even I was getting fed up with hearing my voice going on, never mind the rest of the lads. Then someone suggested putting a bit of music on and Johnny Cash it was. We had played Johnny Cash's 'Ring of Fire' quite a lot in Pakistan before Christmas but in Mumbai it just seemed to hit the spot. All the lads were singing along to it and dancing in the dressing room at lunch-time. Everyone got involved, players and coaching staff as well, and when we walked out for the afternoon session every single player had a big smile on his face. I was bowling the next over and got Rahul Dravid out, and it just carried on from there. That session spurred us on and we claimed a great win on the back of it. The victory in Mumbai in that final Test against India with a young side was a memorable experience for everyone involved. Very few people gave us a chance of getting a result out in India because of the injuries to Michael Vaughan, Simon Jones and Ashley Giles and the absence of Marcus Trescothick, but the team responded brilliantly to chalk up a fantastic victory.

I'm not sure what the Indian team thought about it all. The Test match wasn't in the balance at that stage because they had only lost a couple of wickets. They must have heard our dressing room bouncing up and down and clapping and yee-hahing during the lunch interval. I don't know what they imagined we were up to, but whatever they thought, it worked for us.

News of our use of Johnny Cash's music soon got around — the stump microphone had picked up Geraint Jones singing it as he kept wicket — and it was amazing how the story snowballed. Someone told me there were all sorts of phone-ins about Johnny Cash at home. The song will always remind me of that tour, just as Elton John's 'Rocket Man' always brings back memories of the Ashes. We never plan these team songs. They just surface.

I went through a phase of buying music memorabilia on the internet a few years ago. I have a few signed Elvis records and some U2 and Oasis items that I keep meaning to put up around the house, but I've still not got around to doing it. Some sports memorabilia has found its way into the house as well, but that gets consigned to the gym. You don't want where you live to be a shrine to yourself — that would be very embarrassing. People would come away thinking, 'He likes himself,' and that's just not me. Rachael did insist on putting the BBC Sports Personality of the Year award on the mantelpiece in the living room. Well, it is a great honour and one I was very proud to receive even if I don't go into the living room much.

Victory in Mumbai was worthy of celebration — Andrew Strauss was a happy man, as were we all.

Giving my all with bat and ball for
England in the final Test at Mumbai.

Left: Jimmy Anderson made an impressive return to Test cricket at Mumbai.

Bottom: Rahul Dravid's wicket falls at Mumbai. Music played a key part in our revival during that Test.

The team heads back to the Mumbai dressing room, where the distinctive voice of Johnny Cash rang out once again.

This is my prize for winning man-of-the-match in Mumbai.

Darren Gough and I answering questions during a benefit year event. We were joined on stage by rugby World Cup heroes Martin Johnson and Lawrence Dallaglio.

It seemed a long nervous walk to the stage for my duet with Elton John.

Holly seems to like my guitar playing. I've loved music ever since
I worked on the record counter at Woolworths all those years ago.

CAREER HIGHS AND LOWS

10

Like most sports, cricket is a game of many opinions and I am often asked to name my favourite this, best that and hardest the other. It is difficult to choose between one innings and another, one match and another, and sometimes you change your mind from one week to the next about who or what is your favourite. However after much consideration, I hope I've made the right choices.

My corner of the Lancashire dressing room at Old Trafford is usually a mess. I love the ground because it is where I have grown up.

FAVOURITE GROUND

I suppose my favourite ground in all the world has got to be Old Trafford just because of the emotional attachment I have to it. I have grown up at Old Trafford, ever since I was a little kid, and have enjoyed some of my best moments in cricket there. Old Trafford is where I learned how to play in the nets and where I first made my name. I've also met some of my best friends through playing for Lancashire there — Glen Chapple, Mark Chilton, Paddy McKeown and Neil Fairbrother. The dressing room is like a second home to me. I have my own special area where I dump a lot of my stuff. You should see the shelves above my seat — I've got old bats, sweaters, all sorts of vital junk up there. Old Trafford is also where I played my fiftieth Test, against Australia, and where I enjoyed one of my most satisfying Test wins, against West Indies in 2004. I was particularly pleased with that win because it sealed the series on my home ground, I hit the winning runs and I was batting with my big mate Rob Key at the finish — you can't get much better than that.

Another ground I really enjoy playing at is Lord's. It has an amazing atmosphere about the place and fantastic facilities. The food is good, the dressing room is good, the nets are good — everything about the place is special. I remember the first time I played there, against Zimbabwe, and it was an amazing experience walking out through the Long Room, bat in hand — the only problem was that I was soon walking back after getting 1, so that wasn't too special! Leading the team out as captain against Sri Lanka was a big moment for me. Most people dream of playing at Lord's for their country so to captain England there was a dream fulfilled.

Winning the Test, and with it the series, against West Indies in 2004 is one of my favourite memories of Old Trafford.

Most difficult opponent

I've had the good fortune to play against some of the best cricketers in the present era. I've batted against fast bowlers, including Allan Donald, who bowled very quickly at me early in my Test career, and I've faced Wasim Akram and Brett Lee. I've also bowled against some of the best batsmen, including Sachin Tendulkar, Rahul Dravid, Inzamam-ul-Haq and Ricky Ponting. I would have to say that the toughest opponent I've ever faced though is my old friend Muttiah Muralitharan. The pair of us struck up a really good friendship during his time playing for Lancashire. Murali even flew in from Sri Lanka to attend my wedding to Rachael in 2005, and we went out to eat together on several occasions during the recent Test series against Sri Lanka. However, none of that means I can play him any better than anyone else can.

I rate him as the toughest opponent I've faced simply because when I'm batting against him I just don't know which way the ball is going to go. He's like no other bowler in the world, which is why I rate him so highly. He's unique. He can bowl different deliveries with virtually no change of action. I can probably pick him between 50 and 75 per cent of the time, but he makes you look a right idiot for the other deliveries you can't pick. I suppose the only consolation is that I'm not on my own in finding it difficult batting against him. I'd be worried if I was the only one who couldn't play him, but with his haul of over 600 Test wickets, it's a fairly large club of batsmen who've got out to him.

In addition to being one of my best friends in cricket, Murali is also the most difficult opponent I've faced.

FAVOURITE MATCH I'VE PLAYED IN

This is a really difficult choice because after nearly every victory you think to yourself that nothing can top that, but then you play in another game that does.

I can't ignore the claim of the Second Test against Australia at Edgbaston to be the best match I've ever played in. I can understand why it's been called 'The Greatest Test' because I've never been involved in a match of such drama. It's certainly one of the best Test matches I've played in and it was an added bonus that I did well personally, scoring a half-century in each innings and taking seven wickets in the match.

I've never known tension like it. On that Sunday morning Australia needed 107 more runs to win with only two wickets in hand. The closer they got, the more edgy we all became and, but for a superb delivery from Steve Harmison to remove last man Michael Kasprowicz, they'd have won that Test and probably gone on to win the Ashes.

Acknowledging the crowd after scoring 73 in the second innings against Australia at Edgbaston. What a match that was! I'm not surprised that it has been labelled 'The Greatest Test'.

Brian Lara's record innings of 400 — in the Fourth Test against England in Antigua on 12 April 2004 — took incredible levels of concentration.

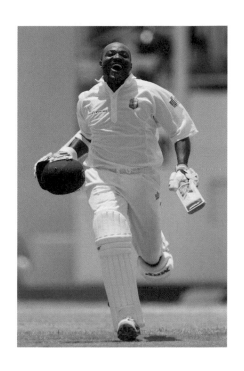

BEST INNINGS I'VE SEEN

A good innings can often depend on the situation. Brian Lara's 400 in Antigua a few years ago was brilliant for his concentration levels and not making a single mistake throughout his innings, but it was also made on a good batting wicket with the series already settled. Other innings also stand out over time, but I still don't think I've ever seen anything as good as Ian Botham's brilliant hundred at Headingley against Australia in 1981. I don't remember watching it on television, but I've watched it on video and it's just incredible. When you consider the state of the match, I don't think you can better it. To follow on in a Test match and then go out and score a brilliant 149 takes some doing. It put England back into the game and Bob Willis grabbed 8/43 to win an amazing Test.

The only other innings that comes close to Beefy's effort was Viv Richards' brilliant 189 against England in a one-day international at Old Trafford in 1984. Once again, I don't remember it at the time but I have seen the videos. Viv was one of my heroes when I was a young lad, mainly because of innings like this one. I liked the way he used to intimidate the bowlers. It was a great thrill for me to talk with Viv at the 2003 World Cup in South Africa about building a one-day innings.

I think you'll have to go a long way to beat Ian Botham's innings at Headingley (left) and Viv Richards' at Old Trafford (top left).

The best bowling performance I've ever seen was Steve Harmison's seven for 12 in Jamaica.

Best bowling performance I've seen

There is no question about the best bowling performance I've seen — Steve Harmison, claiming 7/12 to win the First Test in Jamaica against the West Indies a few years ago. Steve really came of age as a bowler that day. He bowled fast, with lift and movement — I certainly wouldn't have wanted to face him. At one stage, we had every player bar him behind the wicket in catching positions, because his spell was that threatening. His performance gave the whole team a lift and we went on to win the series convincingly.

That display was incredible, but not far behind is Glenn McGrath's performance at Lord's at the start of the 2005 Ashes series. He may not have the pace he once had, but he bowled brilliantly in the conditions and won the game for Australia. We had done well to bowl Australia out for 190 in the first innings and I think the crowd thought we had the game won after that, but he came back and claimed five wickets in the first innings to dismiss us for 155. That first-innings lead played a big part in Australia winning the Test and McGrath came back to claim four wickets more in the second innings. It was an important lesson for a lot of us, and we left Lord's determined not to feel like that again that summer — and we didn't.

I can't talk about great bowling performances without mentioning Muttiah Muralitharan again. I wasn't playing in the game in question, because I'd been dropped for that Test after making my debut earlier that summer, but his performance at The Oval in 1998 to bowl Sri Lanka to victory was incredible. I remember watching him on television taking 16 wickets and confirming what a great bowler he was to become.

Steve Harmison was stunning at Sabina Park (top), but Glenn McGrath bowled superbly at Lord's in the first Ashes Test (bottom).

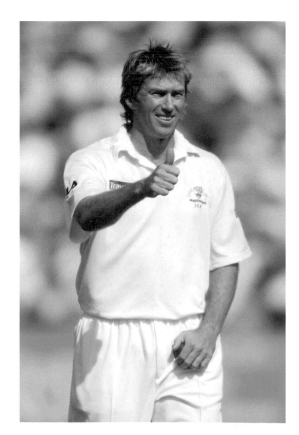

Biggest influence on my career

Any professional sportsman has a number of influences on his career and I am no different. David Lloyd was a big influence at Lancashire during my early days. He guided my career after signing me for the club, and he gave me my Lancashire debut before also giving me my England debuts at Test and one-day international levels.

The biggest influence on my career as a whole would have to be my dad, Colin. His love of cricket was passed on to me and my brother Chris, and it was that passion for the game that led me to where I am today. He was particularly good in the early days, helping to ferry me to all sorts of matches and generally being really supportive. He wasn't one of those dads who push their kids to be the best they can be. He let me play. He gave me plenty of advice and guidance but there was never any pressure on me, and I think that's why I have such a love of the game still. You hear all sorts of stories of sports people giving up because they were put under too much pressure too soon, but that was never the case with me. Dad still comes to as many matches as possible and I think he enjoys it when I do well almost as much as I do.

My parents have always supported me throughout my career. They took over my two dogs when I felt I couldn't give them the time they deserved any more — but I still have visiting rights!

My dad Colin never pushed me when I was younger. He allowed me to play at my own pace and fall in love with the game.

MOST TALENTED YOUNG PLAYER I'VE EVER SEEN

I've played with some outstanding young cricketers. Ben Hollioake always seemed to find the game so easy and Mark Chilton, who is now captain of Lancashire, was also an outstanding young cricketer. The young player I would pick out as the best, though, would be Phil Neville, who has gone on to play football at the highest level for Manchester United, Everton and England.

Phil was a natural all-round sportsman and I am just delighted he chose to sign for United rather than Lancashire. I know I'd have found it a lot harder to make a breakthrough if he had been playing cricket. He was an all-rounder like me, but he bowled quicker and batted better than I did. He was absolutely outstanding and I'm really pleased things worked out for him — in football.

We'll never know how good Ben Hollioake could have been because of his tragic early death. I'll never forget his incredible innings against Australia in that one-day international at Lord's in 1997.

Mark Chilton — a bright prospect in 1997 who has become a popular and successful Lancashire captain.

There is absolutely no doubt that Phil Neville (pictured with brother Gary — Phil's on the left) was the most talented young player I've ever seen. It's just as well for me that Phil was a big success at football — otherwise you might never have heard of me!

FUNNIEST MAN IN CRICKET

That would have to be Anthony McGrath of Yorkshire. He has a fantastic sense of humour and is a real practical joker. You have to be on your guard with him all the time, but he's a great man to have in the dressing room. No matter what the situation, he seems to have the knack of lifting your spirits by making you laugh. I've known him for many years. We played together for the Under-19s and then, of course, he played for England a couple of years ago.

The other person I would pick out is Alex Morris, with whom I also played in the Under-19s. He played for Yorkshire and Hampshire, but had injury troubles with his back. Like McGrath, he is a naturally funny person and very good company. The last time I saw him he was having a beer in the stand at Trent Bridge during the Test against Sri Lanka.

Anthony McGrath (opposite and below left) and Alex Morris are two of the funniest people I've met in cricket.

Biggest disappointment of my career

I've had quite a few disappointments in my career, particularly with England. I remember being very low in India a few years ago when I couldn't score a run, and other times I've been forced to come home early from tours with an injury.

One of my biggest setbacks came not with England but with Lancashire. I've lost my fair share of semi-finals, but I think the Benson and Hedges Cup semi-final defeat by Warwickshire at Old Trafford in 2002 hurt more than any of them. We really thought we were going to win that match, but Warwickshire played well and Neil Carter scored four off the last ball to win the game.

The only other time I've been as low as that was going out of the World Cup in South Africa in 2003. We had a good side, but instead of concentrating on the cricket we seemed to have meeting after meeting about whether we should play our opening match against Zimbabwe or not. We eventually decided against going there as a protest against the political regime and went out because the ICC awarded the points to Zimbabwe. We should probably have gone through to the next stage anyway because we were on top against Australia but lost to them in Port Elizabeth, which ended our World Cup.

Losing the Benson and Hedges Cup semi-final to Warwickshire in 2002 — and seeing their batsman rather than our wicket keeper celebrate — was one of the biggest disappointments of my career.

HIGHLIGHT OF MY CAREER

There can be no doubt about this one — winning the Ashes. I've grown up watching Ashes series and to play in one and win it is something really special. I don't think I'll ever forget those scenes at The Oval after it was all over, with all the crowd celebrating. The whole nation was behind us that summer and nearly all of them seemed to turn out the following day when we had an open-topped bus parade through London. I'm sure those scenes will live with every one of us who was present that day. Playing against the best side in the world and beating them has given us all such a massive boost in confidence. Until you play against the best you are always wondering how you would get on, but that summer we showed what we were made of.

Winning the Ashes has got to be the biggest highlight of my career. The victory parade through London to Trafalgar Square will live in the memory of all who took part.

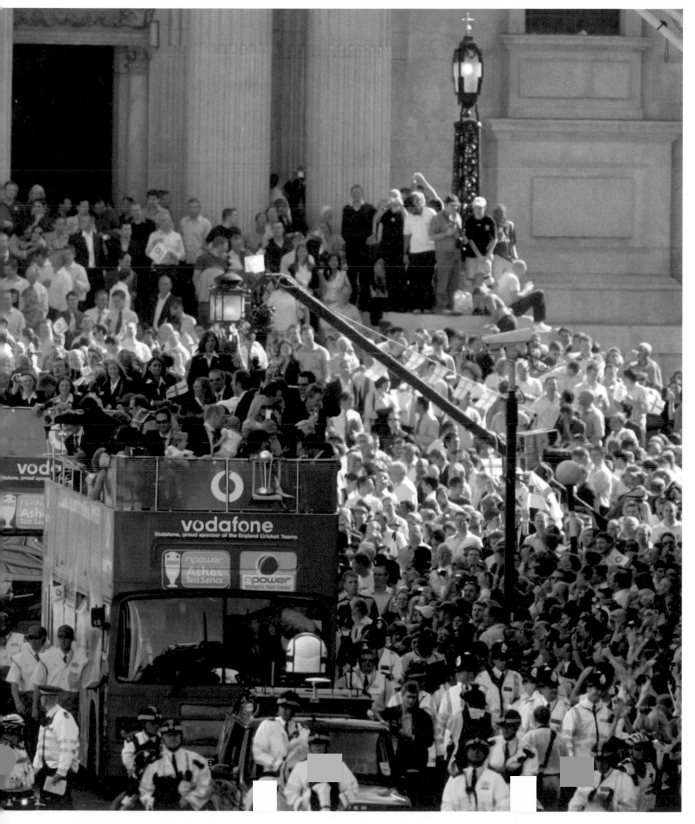

Photographs by Tom Shaw / Getty Images

Additional photographs courtesy of:

Hamish Blair / Getty Images: page 20 above left, 33, 209 centre
Philip Brown: page 47, 60–61, 129, 164, 166, 169 right, 170, 171 right, 173, 174 left, 188, 191 right, 209 above, 215
Clive Brunskill / Getty Images: page 217 above
Graham Chadwick / Getty Images: page 216 left
Andrew Chandler: page 110/111
David Davies / PA / Empics: page 168
Justin Downing / SkySports: page 143 above, centre and below
Justin Downing / SkySports / Rex Features: page 146–147, 148–149
Matt Dunham / AP / Empics: page 20 centre right, 30 above left, 222–223
Mike Finn-Kelcey / Reuters: page 20 above right
Stu Forster / Getty Images: page 21, 167
Getty Images: page 178, 179 above
Tim Graham / Getty Images: page 36 left, 37
Laurence Griffiths / Getty Images: page 92, 93 above and below
David Hartley / Rex Features: page 136, 144–145
Julian Herbert / Getty Images: page 34 above and below, 35, 218 centre
Mike Hewitt / Getty Images: page 206
Ian Jones / Rex Features: page 30 below left
Ian McIlgorm / Rex Features: page 112–113
Tony Marshall / Empics: page 219
Dylan Martinez / Action Images: page 163
Graham Morris: page 214
Indranil Mukherjee / AFP / Getty Images: page 189, 194–195
Adrian Murrell / Getty Images: page 210 above and below, 216 right
Rebecca Naden / PA / Empics: page 53 right, 213 above, 218 left
Mark Nolan / Getty Images: page 31
Ben Radford / Getty Images: page 51 right, 52, 54–55, 192–193
Raveendran / AFP / Getty Images: page 46, 56
Clive Rose / Getty Images: page 211 right
Prakash Singh / AFP / Getty Images: page 190
Michael Steele / Getty Images: page 220
Rui Vieira / PA / Empics: page 209 below
William West / AFP / Getty Images: page 32 left
Simon Wilkinson: page 217 below
Steve Williams / Rex Features: page 179 below
Chris Young / PA / Empics: page 20 below right
Richard Young / Rex Features: page 150

Front cover photograph by Philip Brown
Back cover photograph by Ben Radford / Getty Images